Ask Me Who I Was

iContractor4

Ask Me Who I Was

...audacious brain farts on life, death and immortality

iContractor4

jon m ketcham

Ask Me Who I Was – audacious brain farts on life, death and immortality – iContractor4 **by jon**

© 2018 by **Jon M. Ketcham**. All rights reserved.

No part of this publication may be reproduced or transmitted in any form or by any means, mechanical or electronic, including photocopying and recording, or by any information storage and retrieval system, without permission in writing from author or publisher. The exception would be in the case of brief quotations embodied in the critical articles or reviews and pages where permission is specifically granted by the publisher or author.

Disclaimer: The Publisher and the Author make no representations or warranties with respect to the accuracy or completeness of the contents of this work and specifically disclaim all warranties, including without limitation warranties of fitness for a particular purpose. The fact that an organization or website is referred to in this work as a citation and/or a potential source of further information does not mean that the Publisher or the Author endorses the information the organization or website may provide or recommendations it may make. Further, readers should be aware that internet websites listed in this work may have changed or disappeared between when this work was written and when it is read. Please see following page for additional disclaimer.

ABIYD Publishing Company
www.ABIYD.com

ISBN: 978-0-9905511-4-0 paperback
Library of Congress Control Number: 2018903821

10 9 8 7 6 5 4 3 2 1

Motivational & Inspirational / Metaphysics / Mysticism

First Edition Printed in the United States.

Additional Disclaimer

The information and strategies provided by **Ask Me Who I Was** are intended to educate, inform, empower, amuse and inspire you on your personal journey towards excellence: goal-setting/goal-achieving, growing your business/bank account, achieving optimal health/wellness, improving your relationships and maximizing your quality of life. It is clearly not intended to replace a one-on-one relationship with a licensed health care professional and it is definitely not offered up as a substitute for proper medical or chiropractic advice, diagnosis or treatment. Proper diagnosis and advice relative to treatment of any existing health conditions cannot be made through a book and is well beyond the scope of any information offered. The intent of the author is solely to offer information of a general nature to assist you on your quest for spiritual and emotional well-being. The author will not accept any liability, perceived or otherwise, for the improper application of any principles taught through this text. In the event you, the reader, choose to use or apply any of the strategies in this book for yourself, which is your constitutional right, the publisher and the author assume no responsibility for your actions.

Ask Me Who I Was

Dedication

For Mike

The Native Americans believed that handicapped children were a blessing to their families, the gift of an eternal child. Mike was certainly all that and more to us. When I was a small child, Mike would hold me on his lap and read to me. As I grew from younger brother to legal guardian, he never stopped teaching me, his perpetual and, at times, grumpily impatient student. It seems only fitting that several of the stories in this book revolve around him. I miss you Mike!

Ask Me Who I Was

Table of Contents

Disclaimers   *iv, v*

Dedication   *vii*

Table of Contents   *ix*

Preface   *xiii*

Introduction   *xv*

Section I - The Tribune Articles*   1

Chapter 1   Success   3

Chapter 2   Finding Your Purpose, Getting A Life   7

Chapter 3   Things Cost Too Much   15

Chapter 4   Soulmates   25

Chapter 5   Say Thank You And Get Well Sooner   31

Chapter 6   Living A Life With No Regrets   37

Chapter 7 Transcendental Living:
Journeys Of A Lifetime   41

Chapter 8 What's Your Story?   45

Chapter 9 Soulmates II   49

Chapter 10 Finding Your Afflatus   53

Chapter 11 Finding Inner Peace Without
Caving To Outside Noise   57

Chapter 12 How The Coming Elections
Will Change Your Finances   61

Chapter 13 Awakening Through Change   65

Chapter 14 Roadblocks To Success   67

*BONUS: Tribune Publication Listing   71

Section II - The Blogs   75

Senioritis… Deal With It Now
BEFORE It's Too Late!   77

Where Does Compassion Fit
In Your Approach?   81

Re-thinking Jesus:
Spiritual Food for Thought 83

The 2 Truths Every Expert, Guru,
Influencer, Speaker, Coach, Consultant
& Mentor Know But Won't Likely Tell
You (but probably should!) 85

Caught in the Storm of the "I" 87

Starting Over – Anyone, NOT Everyone,
Can Do Anything 91

Mike's Obituary 95

False Prophets, Ostriches & Groupies –
The Delusions of Social Media
and its Messiahs 97

Dodging the Most Useless Question
in the World – How to Stop Languishing
& Start Living Again 101

Section III - The Talks 103

Failure Talks – A Dual Entendre –
Rising from the Ashes to Dream
Another Dream 105

Perversion, Sin & Death:
The *Dirty* Little Secret That Broke
the Law of Attraction   119

Section IV - The Books   129

The Golden Role – Just Be Nice!   131

The "Zero's Journey" – A Modern-day
Survival Guide to Weathering Accidental
Enlightenment   131

iContractor1 – Constructing Your
Perfect Life by Remodeling YOU
from the Inside-Out!   133

BONUS: Chapter from iContractor1:
Mirrors, Windows, Doors & Light   135

Section V – The Author   145

About the Author   *149*

Connecting to dr. ketcham   *153*

Sources   *155*

Notes   *163*

Preface

As part of a 10-year long collaborative effort by all of the local chiropractors, I used to contribute health-related articles once or twice a year to The Meadville Tribune's monthly HealthBeat column. Then, after submitting an article I had simply titled "Success," I was personally invited by the editor to pen a column of my own, in the forthcoming "Active for Life" quarterly supplement to The Meadville Tribune, and given free reign to philosophize however I chose for the next several years. Those articles, which ran from late 2009 until mid 2013, and were well received in our community, form the basis of this work. Supplemented by a few select blogs, 2 talks and one particularly memorable chapter from my first book, I hope you find it as meaningful to read as I found it to write.

Ask Me Who I Was

Introduction

Identity Crisis – Eating Humble Pie

I currently make my living as the accountant for our local Public Housing Authority. It's not a career that I overtly chose. Rather, it's what I fell back into after my chosen livelihood, chiropractic, completely disintegrated around me following statewide insurance industry changes 6 years ago. When I was initially hired by the Housing Authority, I was forbidden from using my prior title, so as to not confuse the residents and also to insure that my focus was on my new responsibilities and not elsewhere.

I consider myself to be quite extraordinarily blessed, having found this work at the Housing Authority when I did. It enabled me to keep my house, and my marriage too for that matter, after the major loss of my prior career. Furthermore, considering that I had not worked in accounting for nearly 25 years, and I'm not the youngest tool in the shed anymore, getting anyone to take such a chance on me was nothing short of miraculous. Admittedly, the pay is at a fraction of what I had become accustomed to, but it's steady and secure.

I remember once, after having worked at my new job for about a year, my boss asked me, innocently enough I think, "You used to work as a chiropractor. Were you *allowed* to be called 'Doctor' by your patients?" Some might have been bothered by such a question. After all, I once had a thriving, waiting-list chiropractic practice and was fortunate enough to be living my dream life. But, life doesn't always go according to our plans. Rather than dwelling on all I had lost, I was (and still am several years later) profoundly grateful for what I still had and all that this new job had enabled me to salvage. I'm still alive, I still have my home and I'm still married to the love of my life.

"Yes, they used to call me Doctor."

Section I

The Tribune Articles*

Ask Me Who I Was

Chapter 1

Success

"It was the best of times, it was the worst of times…it was the spring of hope, it was the winter of despair; we had everything before us, we had nothing before us, …(1)" So goes the introduction to the classic <u>A Tale Of Two Cities</u> by Charles Dickens. It does not take a rocket scientist to see the parallels to today's economy. With jobs evaporating, companies collapsing and costs increasing exponentially both locally and internationally, times are tough. And yet, I am reminded of a quote by Napoleon Hill that states "Every adversity, every failure…carries with it the seed of an equivalent or greater benefit."(2) Put similarly, Winston Churchill states "The pessimist sees difficulty in every opportunity. The optimist sees opportunity in every difficulty."(3) In other words, no matter how bad it gets, there is always greater opportunity available to any who will seek it and act on it.

Forgive me if I get a bit too scientific for a couple of paragraphs. But, bear with me, and I promise I will bring it all together in the end. While somewhat of an oversimplification, this discussion will help in making my point. In neurophysiology, there is a principle known as the "All-or-Nothing

Principle" and it applies to all normal excitable tissues such as nervous and muscular tissues (neurons and muscle cells). Basically, the All-or-Nothing Principle states that individual excitable tissue cells either depolarize and transmit impulse (in the case of nerve cells) or depolarize and contract (in the case of muscle cells) maximally at 100% or not at all. In other words, if certain minimum threshold conditions are met, they activate completely at 100%. If these minimum threshold conditions are not met, they do nothing!

Each motor neuron (nerve cell) that leaves the spinal cord innervates (powers) many different muscle fibers. All the muscle fibers innervated (powered) by a single motor neuron (nerve cell) are called a motor unit.(4) Changes in strength are not due to how strongly a muscle fiber contracts (remember, it either contracts maximally or not at all), but rather to how many fibers are contracting. In the early weeks of a strength training program, increases in strength are the result of recruitment of more motor units and, subsequently, activation of more muscle fibers.(5)

Still with me? Motivational speaker and success guru Les Brown tells the story about a man who goes for a walk and passes by a house where people are gathered together around a porch. Along with them, the man sees and hears a dog whining and moaning in pain. Curious, and rather concerned, the man approaches the gathering of people and asks "What is wrong with that dog?" "That dog is laying on a nail that has protruded through the floorboard of the porch," he is told. "Then, why doesn't he get up and move to a different spot?" the man asks. "Because it doesn't hurt enough to make him move. It only hurts enough to make him complain," is their reply.(6) How bad does it have to get before you are finally spurred into action, not just complaint?!? Where is your minimum threshold for action?

Once a thought manifests in your mind that you deem worthy of acting upon, your brain triggers a cascade of electro-chemical reactions via the nervous system that activates whatever muscles you need to contract in order to perform the desired action. But, if the minimum threshold level of conditions is not met, nothing happens.(7)

Fear of failure paralyzes and prevents many from ever taking action. Furthermore, prior episodes of failure often damage the self-esteem, causing people to view themselves as less than they really are. Denis Waitley, motivational consultant and trainer to NASA astronauts and Olympic athletes states "You must look at failure as an event, not a person."(8) Many of the world's most successful individuals have come from pasts checkered with failure and bankruptcy. Mark Victor Hansen,

Napoleon Hill, R. Buckminster Fuller, Robert Kiyosaki, Larry King, H.J. Heinz, Milton Hershey, George Foreman, Henry Ford, Meatloaf and Donald Trump all went bankrupt and so did I! Walt Disney went bankrupt so many times that the bankruptcy laws were rewritten stricter in response. Even Abraham Lincoln went bankrupt twice!

Recovery from failure and bankruptcy is much like recovery from physical illness. Often, what occurs is not a steady straight-line recovery. Rather, it is usually a series of 3 steps forward followed by 2-5 steps backward. However, persistence pays dividends. As Frank Zane, 3-time Mr. Olympia states with regard to his training "My training career has been full of new beginnings."(9)

So, when would now be the right time to take action towards a new tomorrow; a better, healthier, more abundant you? How about now?! Now?!?

Chapter 2

Finding Your Purpose, Getting a Life

> "He who has a why to live for can bear with almost any how."
> Nietzsche (1)

More people are unemployed now than at nearly any other time since The Great Depression. Many who are still employed are finding themselves forced to do the work of three for the pay of less than one. Many others are being forced into early retirement and, for those who are not, retirement may appear as the only goal worth pursuing. As more and more baby boomers reach retirement in record numbers, the question that is bound to arise is "Now what?"

Jack LaLanne, known as the Godfather of Fitness, says, "Unless you find another interest, retirement is getting up and going to bed, with eating and television in between." (2) For many of those who are currently unemployed, the scenario is the same. He states further, "statistics indicate that most (people) who retire die within five years of retiring" (2) regardless of the age at retirement!

Some wistfully long for their "glory days" of years past. This often means their high school years.

Regardless of how many years have passed since, nothing again ever meets the "standard of achievement" that was then accomplished; but why? Here are some of my thoughts on this matter. In high school, there is no shortage of interests to provide you with a long list of "mandated" goals to be met. Whether we feel up to the challenges or not, there are a whole army of people from parents to teachers to guidance counselors to coaches to peers to prod us, encourage us, push us, threaten us and so on into becoming more than we feel we can be. However, after graduation, all of this comes to an abrupt end. This can be delayed, somewhat, for those who choose (or are pushed) to pursue a college education. But, even for them, following college graduation, a day of reckoning comes. Unless we learn to set our own goals, follow our own dreams and develop our own sense of purpose, we are left feeling helpless and longing for, even clinging to, the past. This can become a negative habit that is very difficult to break and prevents you from ever moving forward. As Alexander Graham Bell states "Sometimes we stare so long at a door that is closing that we see too late the one that is open." (3) In other words, you will miss all of the opportunities that surround you if you are forever focusing on that which is already past.

This also applies to the unemployed and recently retired. Too often, people become accustomed to having their "goals" given to them by their employers. It is crucial for long-term health and survivability that you learn to set your own continual stream of goals and to develop your own sense of purpose. Whenever a goal is met, you need to have three more waiting in line to take its place. It truly is a matter of life and death. As Barry Bittman, M.D. and Anthony DeFail, M.P.H. state so eloquently in their text <u>Maze of Life</u> "Developing a sense of purpose, taking charge of our own lives and building nurturing relationships strengthen our defenses (against illness)…Every minute of every day, we're in the process of either living or dying. It's simply our choice." (4) Viktor Frankl, a survivor of four WWII concentration camps of the Holocaust, writes with regard to daily prison life "A man who let himself decline because he could not see any future goal found himself occupied with retrospective thoughts…but in robbing the present of its reality there lay a certain danger. It became easy to overlook the opportunities to make something positive of camp life, opportunities which really did exist…they preferred to close their eyes and to live in the past. Life for such people became meaningless…the prisoner who had lost faith in the future – his future – was doomed." (5) There is no power in the past. It can teach you and, hopefully, help you to make better choices in the now, but that is all. Likewise, the future is nothing more than wishful thinking unless appropriate actions are taken in the now to get you to the future you desire. The true power, pregnant with infinite possibilities, exists solely in the now. It is the moment-by-moment choices you make and continue to make that can change everything for you or keep everything the same.

Goals are those short-term targets that we aim for day-to-day, week-to-week, month-to-month and year-to-year. When added up together, they move you towards your purpose or ultimate aim. In the Pixar classic Wall-E, his love interest, a robot on a mission to look for green plant life on earth, refers to her purpose as her "Prime Directive." What a great descriptor that is! Far too many people put more time, thought and effort into planning their vacations than they put into planning out their lives. And, as Jim Rohn, America's Foremost Business Philosopher, states "If you don't design your own life plan, chances are you'll fall into someone else's plan. And guess what they may have planned for you? Not much." (6)

Your hopes and dreams and innermost desires are begging for expression. But guess what? If you never act on your dreams, they die when you die. And, at the risk of sounding like an alarmist, TIME IS RUNNING OUT! In case you haven't figured it out yet, time spares no one. None of us is getting out alive.

If I may, I'd like to offer up a personal example of the importance of goal setting, under the umbrella of purpose. In May of 2001, I found myself on the fourth floor of Meadville Medical Center, hovering between life and death following a ruptured appendix, peritonitis, septicemia and the associated emergency surgeries. Barely alive, unable to move or communicate and connected to life support, I felt as though my whole world had been ripped out from underneath me. This couldn't have just happened to me; I exercised regularly and watched what I ate. In fact, I had just trained down for a bodybuilding show! Angry and scared, knowing this would mean the closing of my office: Bright Spot Chiropractic, I was consumed by feelings of hopelessness. After my breathing tube was removed, I had been instructed to take short walks to re-build my strength and clear my lungs. But, movement was so difficult and required such a psych-up period prior, that I wasn't really interested in participating. Then, one day, an angel of a nurse (one of the many wonderful healthcare workers who cared for me) by the name of Barbara, took my forearms into her hands, looked me in the eyes and said to me "Do you want to live or don't you?!? Then you have to get up and walk!" Then and there, I made the decision to live. What's more, I remembered how, prior to my illness, I had promised my six year old son that I would accompany him on his kindergarten field trip to the Erie Zoo; a field trip that would take place four short weeks following my life-saving surgery. Empowered by my new sense of purpose and specifically wanting to keep my original promise to my son, rolling I-V stand and all, I went walking! After nine days, I was sent home to finish my recovery, open five-inch incision and all. Never did I take my eyes off of my goal, walking a little further every day. Two and a half weeks later, I made it! Even though my incision was still nearly two weeks away from full closure, I was able to keep my promise.

In closing, I'd like to leave you with two quotes, one of my own: "You can't retire from something to nothing and expect to have anything, at least not for very long." And one from Denis Waitley, motivational consultant to NASA, Olympic athletes and others who states: "You've got to have a dream if you want to have a dream come true." (7) Until next time, start making a list of goals / dreams that you feel passionate about accomplishing. Aim for at least 101 or more. If you've never done this before, or not in a very long time, it may seem awkward at first. That's OK. Be patient, sit with a pad and pen, ask yourself "What would I really like to accomplish?" and then write whatever comes to mind. No limitations, no value judgments, just write whatever comes to mind. Also, start thinking about what your purpose is overall. There are no wrong answers here! You decide your purpose, not anybody else. Finally, start considering what actions or activities you will be replacing your prior career or job with to stay healthy. Remember, the human body was designed for motion, not recliners and TV remotes!

Until next time,

Always Believe In Your Dreams!

Ask Me Who I Was

Chapter 3

Things cost too much!

Part I

You don't have to look too far to find people who will agree that things cost too much lately, and prices just keep going up! For those who have recently retired (fixed income) or become unemployed (no income), this may seem even more so. But, what if, hidden within this sentiment is a much subtler truth; a truth which, if understood, could change your whole life?

Jim Rohn, America's Foremost Business Philosopher (recently deceased) tells how he too used to say: "Things cost too much!" Then, his teacher straightened him out on that by saying: "The problem isn't that things cost too much. The problem is that you can't afford it." That's when he finally understood that the problem wasn't cost, the problem was himself! (1)

Effecting real change in your life starts with taking 100% responsibility for your current situation. People are quick to play the victim card, placing blame for their poor situation on the economy, the government, their boss, their spouse, their ex-spouse, their parents, high prices, lack of money, their race, their gender, their age, their education, etc. However, if these truly were the deciding factors, then everybody, similarly situated, would be affected in the same way. Mr. Shoaff, Jim Rohn's teacher, reminds us: "What happens to any of us happens to all of us."(2) Yet, history is replete with examples of people who have managed to prosper in the face of such adversity.

I, personally, have managed to become destitute during some of the most prosperous economic times in history. Because of all that I learned, and the changes that I made in my thoughts, feeling and actions, I also managed to become and remain prosperous during the biggest economic downturn since the Great Depression.

Answering, "How did I contribute to or create my own current situation?" is the first step toward turning things around. George Addair is a successful Arizona businessman who has devoted his life to teaching unique personal development principles to others for more than 30 years. He makes a distinction between outer events (the world around you) and inner states (the world within you). These inner states of being include your wide range of thoughts, feelings and emotions. Basically, Mr. Addair says that everything you experience as the world around you (e.g. your present lifestyle or standard of living) is determined by your inner states of being, not by outer events. (3) The only way to change or influence the outer events you experience is by first changing or taking responsibility for your inner states. This may seem hard to follow (or swallow) initially. However, grasping this one principle dramatically helped turn my life around. As T. Harv Eker, president of Peak Potentials Training states: "Your outer world is simply a reflection of your inner world. If things aren't going well in your outer life, it's because things aren't going well in your inner life. It's that simple."(4)

Dr. Robert Resnick, a psychotherapist in Los Angeles, uses a very simple formula that may make this concept clearer for you. The formula is as follows: E + R = O. Event + Response = Outcome. (5) Of the three variables (E, R, O), your response to any given situation (R) is the **only** variable you have any control over whatsoever! Most people focus their blame on the events (E) for their lack of favorable outcomes (O). But, in the words of Jack Canfield, co-author of the Chicken Soup for the Soul empire, "it is not the external conditions and circumstances that stop you – it is you!...(you) think limiting thoughts and engage in self-defeating behaviors."(5) George Addair states further, "Yes, there are victims in this world but they are victims of themselves."(6)

In other words, every outcome you experience in life (success or failure, health or illness, wealth or poverty, etc.) is a byproduct of how you have responded to prior events, either intentionally or by default. If you want to change your outcomes, change your responses by intentionally changing your thoughts, feelings and emotions. Stedman Graham sums it up by stating, "people who consider themselves victims of circumstances will always remain victims unless they develop a greater vision for their lives."(7)

Bear in mind, there is a time lag between changes in your response and any changes in your outcome. During this time, it may seem like nothing is happening. Stay with it, though, and your success is a given. Jim Rohn tells a wonderful story about a woman who is going through some tough times and struggling to turn her situation around. He describes her as being like a frog in a jar of cream: she keeps kicking and kicking and kicking until, eventually, the milk turns into lumps of butter which enables her to climb out of the jar to freedom.(8) That's a great analogy because that is how change typically comes about. You may feel like you are flailing about for a long time, implementing changes in your internal states of being without any noticeable changes in outcome until, all at once, it snowballs into a new you!

What are some of these changes in internal states of being? For starters, drop out of the "ain't it awful" club. There is far too much whine served there anyways! And, as we all know, too much whine can lead to "aintitawfulism", a chronic, debilitating disease of the heart.

Next time, I will cover in detail an exercise I personally have used with great success for improving my internal state of being. Until then, start looking for ways to respond positively towards the life of your dreams.

Always believe in your dreams!

Ask Me Who I Was

Part II

Last time, we talked about how our response to the events around us actually creates our outcomes. This month, as promised, I would like to share an exercise that I have used to great success towards improving the outcomes in my life.

One way in which I improved my internal state of being involved the nature and orientation of my thoughts. Rather than focusing on the past (glory days) or the present (how bad it was at the time), I spent time creating pictures in my mind of how I would like my ideal life to look. I devoted time, daily, to this exercise and really put a lot of heart into it. Peter Daniels, one of the richest men in Australia, performs a similar exercise and credits it with turning his life around. In fact, Mr. Daniels devotes an entire day a week just to thinking and visualizing his tomorrows. Interestingly, he has the dubious distinction of having gone broke three times within five years before turning his life around. For the record, I went broke three times within four years, but I always was an overachiever! Einstein used a similar strategy, actually doing his pondering in a special thinking chair. (9) Viktor Frankl, a survivor of four WWII concentration camps of the Holocaust, survived in part due to his ability to paint mental pictures of a better tomorrow. He spent considerable time visualizing himself successfully practicing psychology, lecturing, attending concerts and enjoying a fulfilling lifestyle, all of which actually came to pass following his release. (10)

Here is the thinking / visualizing exercise as I perform it:

Look at your life as though it is a play which you are writing / scripting through your thoughts, feelings, emotions, expectations and actions. You write the script. You hold the casting calls. You attract all of the players.

Everyone and everything that you encounter in your life is there because you attracted / scripted it. Everyone and everything plays their role 100% perfectly according to the script you have written. If you don't like a particular act, re-write / re-script it! You don't get to choose who will fill which roles. You merely write the script and the perfect actors show up in the perfect scenery. Anyone / anything that plays or played a role you dislike is still performing 100% perfectly according to the script you previously wrote. If you don't like the role they play or played, change your script (i.e. your thoughts, feelings, expectations, etc.). Further, you don't have to invite any particular actors back for a repeat or an encore performance. Change the script. Again, you can not control who will fill which roles. All you can do is re-write the script to include new or different roles.

Your subconscious mind can not tell the difference between current events and future, imagined events. This is where the magic of visualization springs from. However, it also can not tell the difference between current events and past events. Every time you re-live a past hurt, a past perceived failure, you resuscitate it and give it life anew. If you want to create real, lasting change in your life, stop re-animating (re-living) past hurts and start re-scripting (visualizing) new successes.

One way you might apply this exercise and make it more meaningful is to write an annual newsletter about your life and all you have accomplished in a year. But, remember, write it as though it has already happened, one year in advance!

Concerning your thoughts, feelings and actions, I would like to close with a quote from motivational speaker Zig Ziglar, "You are free to choose, but the choices you make today will determine what you will have, be and do in the tomorrow of your life." (11) Choose wisely!

Ask Me Who I Was

Chapter 4

Soulmates

My wife Lisa and I share a rather unusual level of closeness. We do everything together. We work together (she is the office manager of my chiropractic practice), we play together, we parent together, we even share a single car together (and have for the past seven years). While some might find the amount of time we spend together excessive, I could not imagine life any other way. Lisa completes me in every way and truly is the love of my life. Some might even say that we are soulmates. What exactly is a soulmate anyways? Strictly speaking, a soulmate is the one(s) who resonates perfectly with your soul. However, it is my opinion that everyone you are attracted to and connect with resonates (or resonated) with who you are (or were) at that time. Not only that, but I would go so far as to say that they resonate (or resonated) 100% perfectly with who you are (or were) at any given moment in time. We are always finding our ideal mates. It's just that the one(s) who are ideal for us at any given time are not always to our liking. Therefore, if you want to find your "ideal" soulmate, according to how you choose to define them, you must first become the match to that which you seek. If you are not satisfied with whom you have been finding, then you need to up-level your own soul development first!

Often times, people will move to a new locale to get a "new start" only to find that they are plagued by the exact same problems as before. The reason is, wherever you go, there **you** are! This also explains why some people keep ending up in bad relationships with similar personality types who have certain quirks or dysfunctions. Until you change who you are on the inside, you will keep encountering the same themes, no matter where you move. In the words of motivational speaker Les Brown, "You don't get in life what you want. You get what you are." (1) Finding and attracting your "ideal" soulmate has far more to do with who you be (your level of being) than what you do!

When I reached the point in my own personal development that I wanted to find my "ideal" soulmate, rather than just settle for whomever was available at any given time, I created a three-step process that went like this:

First, I sat down and thought about exactly what traits, qualities, etc. my ideal soulmate would have. In this way, I figured I would be better able to recognize her (or not her) when she arrived. Initially, this process began by stating what trait, qualities, etc. I did not want. Most people have been in a bad relationship or three, so it's usually easier to begin there. Just remember, the negatives (what you don't want) are your starting point, not your ending point. After re-stating / re-formulating my wants into the positives (what I did want), I wrote them down in as much detail as possible.

Second, and this is the biggest one, I set about developing those same traits in myself that I wished to find in another. Intuitively, I knew that like *reflects* like. Therefore, I felt it unrealistic to expect to receive from another that which I was unable to first give out. So, the process of personal development began. I truly strove to be the person my dog thought I was when he would greet me each day after work!

Finally, I set about pursuing those activities I had always had "on hold until someday when I find my true love." I had always wanted to compete in bodybuilding competitions and felt that "someday", with the right woman beside me, I would be able to pursue such. So, I picked a competition twelve weeks away and started training for it. Four weeks out from show, I met Lisa! This last step is the ultimate act of faith, acting "as if" you already have found that which you seek. Consistency and congruency are the key. For example, seeking your true love while simultaneously engaging in one-night stands is not congruent. The very act of going out, trolling for whomever you can find, sends a very different message than wanting to find your true love. Hopefully, you wouldn't engage in these behaviors if you were already in a loving, committed relationship with your true soulmate. Acting how you would act if you already had your ideal love in your life is the key.

Those already partnered with someone, but not satisfied with their relationship can instantly up-level it by working on themselves, improving who they be on the inside.

Summarizing this 3-step process:

1) **Decide** – exactly what does your ideal love look like? Put it in writing. State it in the affirmative only (what you want, not what you don't want).

2) **Change who you be (your level of being)** – develop those same traits in yourself that you wish to find in another. Remember, like *reflects* like.

3) **Act "as if"** – what would you be doing if you already had your ideal mate beside you?

By the way, Lisa and I have been together through the good (success & prosperity), the bad (going broke 3x in 4 years) and the ugly (my near fatal appendix rupture) for nearly twenty years now and she still makes it all worthwhile!!!

Ask Me Who I Was

Chapter 5

Say, "Thank You" and Get Well Sooner: The Healing Power of Positive Emotions

> "Every adversity... carries with it the Seed of an equivalent or a greater Benefit." Napoleon Hill (1)

One of the primary reasons prompting people to seek care from their physicians is the onset of pain. This is true across the board for all health care professions. Patients often show up on their doctor's doorstep with a panic-laden "fix me!" emblazoned across their pain-induced expressions. But, what if, as Napoleon Hill states, there is a seed of an equivalent or greater benefit hidden within their malady?

When we are in pain, we experience contracture in our physiology. Muscular contraction and muscle guarding leads to spasm and trigger point formation. Byproducts of this prolonged muscle activity (e.g. lactic acid) serve to self-perpetuate the cycle of unrelenting muscle activity. Increases in sympathetic nervous system activity (the stress response) cause cardiovascular contracture resulting in increases in both heart rate and blood pressure. Furthermore, gastric contracture causes indigestion and nausea while intestinal contracture leads to constipation and/or diarrhea. Immunologic contracture results in immuno-suppression. Meanwhile, all of the above contractures serve to magnify the pain, forcing the patient into a more self-absorbed state of mind.

Breakthroughs in awareness concerning the lack of any true distinction between mind and body have led to some very interesting and creative approaches to bringing a patient back to wholeness or wellness. <u>The Stress of Life</u>, written by Hans Selye in the 1920s, detailed the vast negative effects of the negative emotions on body chemistry. O. Carl Simonton, M.D. writes in <u>Getting Well Again</u> how "chronic stress results in a suppression of the immune system" (2) and further reports "the physician Galen, writing nearly 2000 years ago, observed that cheerful women were less prone to cancer than were women of a depressed nature." (3) More recent studies out of Ohio University showed that blisters healed 40% slower in those exposed to negative emotions compared to those exposed to neutral ones. (4) In other words, negative emotions produce negative biochemical changes in the body whereas positive emotions produce positive biochemical changes.

Anyone familiar with the Law of Reflection knows that whatever you focus on expands. Wherever attention goes, energy flows, like shining a flashlight into the darkness. Patients who become completely focused on what's wrong with themselves and all of their symptoms actually help to perpetuate their situation. Because we all have the power to choose where we focus our attention, to choose our thoughts, we can choose to shift our attention away from being sick to being well. Dr. John Hagelin, a world-renowned quantum physicist, states: "Happier thoughts lead to essentially a happier biochemistry. A happier, healthier body...our thoughts and emotions are continuously reassembling, reorganizing, recreating our body." (5)

While certainly a distinction must be made between the need for, or not the need for, crisis care, this does open up some interesting possibilities for improving your recovery. Obviously, in a crisis situation, that is the time for emergency room care. No amount of positive mental energy is going to adequately offset the need for crisis intervention once the limitations of matter have been exceeded. For instance, if you experience sudden onset chest pain, go to the emergency room! However, in more minor, non-life threatening situations, you can give this a try.

Just like you have to have light to have dark and loud to have quiet, there are both positive and negative emotions. Negative emotions include fear, hate, worry, intolerance, judgment, hopelessness and depression. Like pain, all negative emotions cause a contraction of your physiology. Positive emotions, on the other hand, expand your physiology. Positive emotions include gratitude, acceptance, love, joy, hope and optimism. Positive emotions and negative emotions cannot co-exist, one replaces the other. Therein lies the beauty. By choosing to focus your energy on one, it automatically replaces the other. This is why sugar pills work (aka the placebo effect). They replace negative emotions with hope. As stated before, negative emotions cannot coexist in the presence of hope. As the body shifts from contraction to expansion, on a multitude of levels, the healing process begins.

Probably the easiest way to implement this strategy to health is by making the practice of uncommon appreciation, or gratitude, a way of life. Everyone can find something to be thankful for in their lives. There is a wall plaque in my home that says, "Contentment is not the fulfillment of what you want, but the realization of how much you already have." I would go one step further and state, Health is not the restoration of what you lack, but the realization (and gratitude for) how much wellness you already have! At the very least, if you haven't got all the thing you want, be grateful for the things you don't have that you don't want. Bottom line, find something in your life to be grateful for, focus on that, expand your physiology and get well sooner!

As O. Carl Simonton, M.D. states, "the body is demanding attention in the only way it knows how…illness is an opportunity for the individual to achieve emotional growth." (6)

Ask Me Who I Was

Chapter 6

Living A Life With No Regrets

> "The average person goes to his grave with his music still in him."
> Oliver Wendell Holmes (1)

In his classic work, <u>Illusions: The Adventures of a Reluctant Messiah</u>, Richard Bach states, "You are never given a wish without also being given the power to make it true. You may have to work for it, however." (2) Jim Rohn, America's Leading Business Authority On Success, says, "We must all suffer from one of two pains: the pain of discipline or the pain of regret. The difference is discipline weighs ounces while regret weighs tons." (3)

    Most of us start life starry-eyed, full to the brim with dreams, hopes and aspirations. Unfortunately, the realities of life have a way of setting in, chipping away at and eroding our dreams. Some, perhaps most, give up their dreams, at least "temporarily" to: raise a family, pay the bills, follow a career, not upset another (spouse, parent, teacher, etc.) and on and on. Before you know it, decades may have passed. Every major life transition such as marriage, divorce, job loss, illness, retirement and loss of a spouse or loved one tends to re-connect us with our inner longings, begging the question: When would NOW be a good time to resuscitate those dreams? How about you? If you knew for certain you would die tomorrow, could you honestly say you would do so without any regrets? Or, is there still something, deep within you, yearning for expression, burning to get done?

Long-term survival rates for some of the more serious ailments (think: cancer) are highest among those who are able to re-frame their illness as a positive experience more than just a negative one; the "best worst" experience of their lives, so to speak. Finding the rose among the thorns is no easy task, initially. But, it can be done. As Napoleon Hill states in <u>Think And Grow Rich</u>, "Every adversity... carries with it the seed of an equivalent or a greater benefit." (4) One of the biggest potential benefits of a major illness is that it forces some to take action. So many put their hopes, dreams, needs, etc. "on hold" until "someday." When they become ill, it brings "someday" into the NOW.

A few years back, Jack Nicholson and Morgan Freeman starred in a wonderful movie called "The Bucket List." Faced with only six months to a year left to live, they compile a "bucket list," a list of things they want to do, see and experience before they "kick the bucket." Basically, it is a written listing of their innermost dreams and longings. They could have written and pursued their "bucket lists" at any time in their lives up until that point, but never did. Only when faced with the near certainty of imminent death did writing and accomplishing a bucket list seem important. Near the end of the movie, one of the actors acknowledges having "lived" more in what turned out to be the final three months of their lives than either had done in their entire lives up until that point.

By choosing to honor their spirit and follow their innermost passions for those three months, they finally were saying: 1. "I matter." 2. "My dreams matter." 3. "I am following my dreams because I am worth it!" How different would your life be if you said (and meant) those same three statements to yourself?

Wayne Dyer states, "You'll seldom experience regret for anything that you've done. It is what you haven't done that will torment you." (5) As my wife Lisa says, "Regret is a self-inflicted prison on the soul." Only by honoring our innermost longings can we be complete. The discipline it takes to follow your dreams is nothing compared to the regret you will feel if you don't. It shouldn't take a terminal illness to motivate you to take action. You do matter! Your dreams matter! Follow your dreams now because you are worth it! The time to resuscitate your dreams is NOW. Don't let it pass you by!

Ask Me Who I Was

Chapter 7

Transcendental Living:
Journeys of a Lifetime

Tran•scen•den•tal – adj.:   1.) going beyond ordinary limits; surpassing
2.) being beyond ordinary or common experience, thought or belief (1)

On April 16th, 2011 athletes from as far away as Alabama, New York and Ohio, as well as numerous local athletes, converged on Saegertown Jr./Sr. High School's auditorium stage to compete in the inaugural run of "The Reach for The Ring", a drug-tested Bodybuilding, Figure and Bikini Championship. Many months of arduous preparation went into getting each and every one of the athletes, who ranged in age from early twenties to late sixties, ready for the stage. And, while only a select few earned top honors and the elusive Pro card, every one of the athletes overcame tremendous obstacles and odds just to be there.

Randall J. Strossen, editor-in-chief of Milo: A Journal For Serious Strength Athletes, coined a wonderful term: "Transcendental Levitation." (2) Basically, he says that when evaluating the results of any weight-training regimen, whether for bodybuilding, powerlifting, Olympic lifting, strongman, Highland Games or just general fitness, the real value comes as a result of the process itself. Goal-setting / goal-getting, striving and overcoming obstacles changes you; so much so that who you become in the process far exceeds the original goal or intent. Hence, the transformative power of the struggles against gravity up-levels you not just physically, but mentally and spiritually as well: "Transcendental Levitation!"

A similar phenomenon often follows serious illness or failure (e.g. bankruptcy). Both illness and failure have a way of forcibly stripping away all of our false personas and defense mechanisms; laying bare for all the world to see, our weaknesses, frailties and shortcomings. These events, and how we choose to respond to them, provide an opportunity for us to re-connect with our inner, higher selves. Pondering the questions: "Who am I? Why am I here? What do I stand for?" begins the process of re-claiming your true self; "Transcendental Reclamation", if you will. Honoring your innermost needs and desires up-levels your level of being and provides inspiration and example for others. Consider people like Gandhi, Mother Teresa, Martin Luther King and His Holiness the Dalai Lama.

Every one of us matters. It's up to each one of us, individually, to decide why. Mother Teresa states, "Each of us feels that we are just a drop in the ocean, but the ocean would be less without that missing drop." (3)

It is not necessary to lift weights or become ill or fail at something to improve oneself or transcend one's current level of being. (Although, I do have experience with all three!) Jim Rohn, America's Leading Business Authority, says that one of the greatest lessons he ever learned was when his mentor told him to "set a goal of becoming a millionaire for what it will make of you to achieve it. Set a goal that will make you reach for the stars." (4) He goes on to say, "the greatest value in life is not what you *obtain*, the greatest value in life is what you *become* along the way." (5) Part of what makes goal-setting / goal-getting, striving and overcoming obstacles so powerful and so transformative is the leap of faith that it requires us to make. None of us knows for sure, upon embarking on any new journey, what the outcome will be. As such, it requires us to believe in ourselves, often well in advance of any concrete evidence in favor of such. In doing so, we catch glimmers of our own unlimited potential. Furthermore, the "distraction" of goal-setting / goal-getting, striving and overcoming obstacles gets us out of our own way. This process connects people, sometimes for the first time ever, with the feeling of their own intrinsic worth.

So many people spend their whole lives trying to fit in, to be like everybody else, and not make waves. But, as I often say, conformity is the death knell to success. We come in all shapes, sizes, colors and orientations and that is part of the beauty of being human. Trying to fit everyone into the same mold robs us of our own unique contribution to society.

Any time we base our self-worth or value as a human being on our appearances, or worse, someone else's opinion of our appearance, we are in trouble. You have value just because you are! The real value in goal-setting / goal-getting, striving and overcoming obstacles comes as a direct result of the process itself. By persevering against the odds, you get a glimpse of your true worth and inner power as a human being: "Transcendental Realization". As Neale Donald Walsch, author of the <u>Conversations With God</u> book series states, "I have learned to trust the process of life , and not so much the outcome. Destinations have not nearly as much value as journeys." (6)

Chapter 8

What's Your Story?

> "All stories, even one's we love, must eventually come to an end. And, when they do, it's only an opportunity for another story to begin."
> Eric Applebaum, The Hat Collector (1)

Back in the early 1800s, people thought that you could assess a person's personality and character by examining the shape and size of various parts of their skull; a pseudoscience known as Phrenology. Similarly, the ancient Greek philosophers thought that you could assess a person's personality and character by evaluating various facial traits; a study known as Physiognomy. Palmistry, or Chiromancy, is the attempt at characterization and foretelling the future through the study of the palm, or palm reading, and has been traced back to ancient Greece as well. And, through an ancient practice known as Tasseography, residual patterns made by tea leaves or coffee grounds are evaluated to provide insight into the subconscious and foretell the future. I don't profess to know much about any of these practices. However, I do know that you can learn an awful lot about a person by listening to the stories that they tell about themselves.

Every one of us is an amalgamation of the thoughts and experiences of our lifetime. The stories we tell others about ourselves can provide tremendous insight into who we are and where we are headed. If we are constantly telling others, "I'm too _____ (old, young, fat, skinny, poor, etc.)", we broadcast to those around us what our self-image and perceived personal flaws are. Similarly, always stating, "I can't afford _____ (fill in the blank)", rather than considering "How can I?", reveals our lack and limitation mindset.

Motivational speaker and success guru Les Brown says that most people only go so far in life and then they "park" because the story that is playing in their head says, "This is it." (2) This is problematic for a number of reasons. For one thing, such self-imposed limitations prevent us from ever reaching our full potential. Far more compelling, however, is the thought that life is a continuum. We are not static beings. In other words, we are always either moving towards or away from our perceived ideals. As soon as we stop striving to be our best we start gravitating toward being our worst! Motivational speaker Steve Duncanson said this, "Life is a fight for territory and once you stop fighting for what you want, what you don't want will automatically take over." (3) Jim Rohn, America's Foremost Business Philosopher (recently deceased) says, "We must all wage an intense, lifelong battle against the constant downward pull. If we relax, the bugs and the weeds of negativity will move into the garden and take away everything of value." (4)

This all becomes infinitely more important when we reach milestones such as graduation, marriage and retirement. I've written previously about the need for setting new goals to take the place of old or accomplished ones. [Active For Life 1/30/2010 & 4/28/2010: "Finding Your Purpose, Getting A Life"; "Active For Life 4/27/2011: "Living A Life With No Regrets"] Only by having a never-ending stream of goals are we prompted to constantly strive to be our very best rather than settling and resting on our laurels. The story you tell yourself that "This is it" must be relegated to the fiction that it is.

With all of the negativity in the news concerning the economy, politics, unemployment and crime, it is easy to let that become a part of your story as well. Maybe it's time for a new story, a positive one. Reaching milestones, both positive (graduation, marriage, promotion, retirement) and negative (divorce, unemployment, loss of a spouse or loved one) doesn't have to be the end of your story.

Edit your story to be the way you wish it to be. Find compelling reasons to drive you to get out of bed every morning. Only let the positive news in and only speak the positive out. Anything that does not serve you should be edited out of your thoughts and words. And, when you find yourself at a milestone, write another chapter, write another volume, write a whole new series of volumes! Just don't let yourself go out of print. You decide!

Chapter 9

Soulmates II

"How little do we know that which we are! How less what we may be!"
Lord Byron (Don Juan) (1)

Due to the immense popularity of our article Soulmates [originally published in The Meadville Tribune's Active For Life supplement and titled: "Steps to avoid looming loneliness of retirement" 1/29/2011] and with Valentine's Day right around the corner, this seemed like the perfect time to revisit the topic of love at any age with Soulmates II. For those of you still floundering in the game of love, prepare to have your world rocked! Whether you are still seeking your "ideal" soulmate or maybe you are just looking to improve the relationship you are already in, help is at hand.

Back in the time of ancient Greece (400 BC), Plato quotes Socrates as having stated the long-established wisdom of the time, "Know thyself." In fact, "know thyself" was a central component of the philosophy of Socrates. How many of you today can honestly claim to know yourselves? Many never bother to consider such a monumental task. Fortunate indeed is the individual, whether due to illness, orientation or calamity who is forced early on in life to ponder such a magnificent series of deep questions such as 'Who am I?', 'What do I stand for?', 'What is my purpose?' and then, ultimately, 'What do I want?' How do you ever expect to recognize your "ideal" soulmate when they show up in your life if you never bothered to define them in the first place? If you went out to a restaurant to eat, how would you ever expect to recognize your meal, or for that matter ever receive it in the first place, if you didn't first DECIDE precisely what you wanted and then place you order?!?

After deciding precisely who or what you are looking for, the next step is learning to love yourself. In any relationship, existing or desired, you must work on yourself first (and only!). If you don't love yourself, neither will anyone else. If you don't respect yourself, why would anyone else? Improving your feelings of self-worth is like amassing "desire-ability" income. As your self-worth increases, you become more desirable to others. Don't confuse this with false bravado, bragging and ego however. What we are talking about here is a genuine feeling of love and appreciation for yourself as you already are; your likes and dislikes, the good, the bad and the ugly!

Finally, it is imperative that you stop "searching" for your "ideal" soulmate and instead, start "BECOMING" that which you seek. Rather than chasing after someone or something external to yourself, seek to become someone worthy of love! In other words, instead of looking "outside" yourself for love, start by improving or up-leveling "within" yourself. If you want to find your perfect love, then you must strive to become perfectly lovable.

> **"If you would be loved,
> love and be lovable."
> Ben Franklin (2)**

In summary, seek first to know yourself. Then, seek to love yourself. Finally, seek to improve yourself. All of us are familiar with 'to do' lists. If you are seeking your "ideal" soulmate, maybe it's time to create a 'to be' list! As my Facebook friend Cristie Crit Johnson says, "A 'to be' list is as important as a 'to do' list!"

Ask Me Who I Was

Chapter 10

Finding Your Afflatus

Have you ever had one of those serendipitous moments where, while looking for one thing, you accidently stumble across something even more valuable? This happened to me one day while I was looking up a word in the dictionary. I'm not even sure what that original word was now. But the word I stumbled across by accident has stayed with me to this day. It is one of the most beautiful words I have ever come to know. That word is "afflatus." Webster's New Universal Unabridged Dictionary (1996) defines afflatus as:

    (1.)inspiration; an impelling mental force acting from within

    (2.)divine communication of knowledge (1)

Now, you may be saying to yourself, "so what's the big deal about afflatus?" Let me ask you something. Why do you get out of bed every day? What motivates you to get up and go to work? Is it just so you can pay your bills; a means to an end? Is it peer pressure; worrying about what others will think of you if you fail to conform to societal norms? Maybe it's out of sheer boredom; nothing else better to do? As Jim Rohn says, "If you don't design your own life plan, chances are you'll fall into someone else's plan. And guess what they may have planned for you? Not much." (2) Do you even have a definite plan for your life?

> **"He who has a why to live for can bear with almost any how."**
> **Nietzsche (3)**

All of us are blessed from birth with an inner cache of dreams and aspirations. When we are young, we literally overflow with the abundance of these dreams. However, as we "mature", quite often these dreams and aspirations get suppressed, squashed and placed on perpetual "hold" mode. Instead, as we lower our ambitions, we set more "reasonable" and "realistic" goals.

> **"The greater danger for most of us lies not in setting our aim too high and falling short; but in setting our aim too low, and achieving our mark."**
> **Michelangelo (4)**

What is holding you back right now from living your dream life? Is it a fear of failure? Or, just maybe, is it really a fear of success? Marianne Williamson says, "Our deepest fear is not that we are inadequate. Our deepest fear is that we are powerful beyond measure. It is our light, not our darkness that frightens us." (5)

What if you knew that you could not fail? How would you plan your life differently? Would you finally be willing to take your life off of hold and follow your dreams? As I state in my book *iContractor1...Constructing Your Perfect Life By Remodeling YOU From The Inside-Out*, "Your dreams are your gifts from God. Following those dreams is your gift to God." (6) Your dreams are not meant to be just for you. Your dreams are for the benefit of all of humanity. Marianne Williamson continues, all of us "were born to make manifest the glory of God that is within us. It's not just in some of us, it's in everyone. And as we let our own light shine, we unconsciously give other people permission to do the same." (7)

Which begs the question, have you found YOUR afflatus yet?!?

Ask Me Who I Was

Chapter 11

Finding Inner Peace Without Caving To Outside Noise!

In biology, molting is a process whereby an animal such as a snake will shed their old skin once it gets too tight for them. As it outgrows their old skin, a snake will be compelled to rub their head against rough surfaces, causing the already stretched skin to split and peel backwards on itself, similar to taking your socks off inside-out, until the snake can then crawl out entirely. This process repeats on a regular basis as the snake continues to mature and grow. (1) How many of you could honestly profess to being comfortable in your own skin? Judging from the surging popularity of cosmetic surgeries, weight-loss supplements, extreme exercise programs and the like, I would venture to say that it is very few indeed!

So many of us live our lives based around worrying about what other people will think of us. But, according to Dr. Daniel Amen, psychologist and author of Change Your Brain, Change Your Life, they may not be thinking of you as much as you like to think! Dr. Amen refers to what he calls the "18/40/60 Rule" which goes as follows: at age 18, you worry about what everybody thinks of you; at age 40, you don't care what anybody thinks of you; at age 60, you realize that nobody was thinking that much of you anyways! (2)

> **"Someone's opinion of you does not have to become your reality."**
> **Les Brown (3)**

In other words (mine, actually), during Stage I (age 18), we are seeking approval from others. We are wanting to comply and conform to the wishes and expectations of others. During Stage II (age 40), we begin to live our lives in defiance of the wishes and expectations of others. We rebel. Finally, during Stage III (age 60), we begin to live our lives solely for ourselves. This is not a selfish stage; rather, it is about finally being true to who we are. Recognizing our own mortality, we begin to take our lives off of hold and listen to our own inner longings.

While the "18/40/60 Rule" is a good "rule of thumb," many never make it past Stage II (age 40). In fact, some don't even make it past Stage I (age 18). There is an old African proverb that states, "If there's no enemy within, the enemy outside can do you no harm." (4) Who would/could you be if you made the shift TODAY to Stage III?!? Who are you really? Do you even really know?

There are actually 2 prongs to this: being who you are AND allowing others to be who they are; not pressuring others to conform to our ideals or spurring their rebellion by our attempts. Are you secure enough in who you are to allow others to be who they are? In self-acceptance, and subsequent acceptance of others as they already are, lies the key to centering our lives and making ALL of our dreams come true! Just remember, no one will value you until you value yourself! Likewise, no one can truly love you until you love yourself. So, how about it?

Ask Me Who I Was

Chapter 12

How the coming Presidential election will change your finances!

"Can anybody remember when times were not hard and money not scarce?"
Ralph Waldo Emerson (1803-1882) (1)

When I was 16 years of age, my mother passed away following a long, valiantly fought battle with cancer. Being a "momma's boy" in every sense of the word, I suddenly found myself alone and unprepared for the harsh realities that were my new existence. While I won't profess to being a particularly quick learner, it did not take too terribly long for me to realize that nobody else was going to coddle and baby me, like my mother had, anymore. So, I picked myself up, dusted myself off and ventured tentatively into my new reality. At first, I felt frightened, alone and woefully inadequate. However, as I grew in both confidence and capability, the inevitable result of taking responsibility for one's own situation in life, a whole new world of possibilities unfolded before me.

Today's tumultuous economy has many feeling similarly to how I did at 16: frightened, alone and woefully inadequate. Faced with corporate downsizing, job loss, early retirement, Medicare cutbacks and the like, all of which are compounded by the ever increasing disparity between income levels and the rising cost of living, many find themselves looking outside of themselves for the solution.

Thus, as we near another presidential election, multitudes are hoping that the results of this year's election will be the catalyst needed to turn the economy around and bring an end to their individual economic blight. Many subject themselves to further unnecessary stress as they attempt to shoulder the responsibility for events and circumstances outside of their immediate control, like the economy, because they feel so powerless to change anything. Jim Rohn, "America's Foremost Business Philosopher"(now deceased), used to have what he called his "not much" list. (2) For instance, if the Democrats succeed in retaining the White House next month, how much will your personal economic situation likely change in the coming months? "Not much!" And, if the Republicans succeed in winning the White House next month, how much will your personal economic situation likely change? "Not much!"

By focusing on all that they cannot really change, people tend to not even be aware of the one thing that they can change: their attitude, their response; the one thing that is the only thing! The only way the economy is going to improve is the same (and only) way society is going to improve: one person at a time! And it starts with each and every one of you, on the inside, from the inside-out. Things won't improve by looking to the President to solve it all. Things won't ever improve by looking to sources outside yourself to solve them. Improving you is the solution.

Start by focusing on what you can control. The only variable you ever have any real control over whatsoever is yourself; and, of that, really only over your attitude of mind. Viktor Frankl, a survivor of four WWII concentration camps of the Holocaust, wrote in <u>Man's Search For Meaning</u>, "Everything can be taken from a man but one thing: the last of the human freedoms – to choose one's attitude in any given set of circumstances, to choose one's own way." (3) You get to choose your response to any and every given situation.

The key to turning around the economy and the nation rests squarely between each and every one of your shoulders, in your hearts and minds! Now, don't get me wrong, I am not saying that your vote does not count next month. It does. But, once you have placed your vote, get to work on you. The one thing, which is the ONLY thing, you have control over is your attitude of mind... and that is the ONLY thing you need to change in order to change EVERYTHING!

Ask Me Who I Was

Chapter 13

Awakening Through Change

The nature of life is change. And, the more we strive to keep things the same, the greater the changes seem to be. Nothing lasts forever. We only need to visit any cemetery to get a fresh reminder of the transient nature of our existence. Economies and industries rise and fall. Remember Kodak film? How about the local industries of Talon zippers and, more recently, Tool and Die? Even Chiropractic is not immune to change. It is a given that, at some point in time, in each one of our lives, we will all experience the bitter taste of failure as well as the savory sweetness of success; the vulnerability of weakness as well as the gift of inner strength; the fragility of illness as well as the radiance of health; the emptiness of abandonment as well as the nourishment of love; the paralyzing effects of fear as well as the faith-building effects of courage; the poverty of ignorance as well as the wellspring of new knowledge. Of course, we all hope to spend most of our days on the right-hand side of this equation, basking in abundant success, strength, health, love, courage and knowledge. However, the only guarantee in life is that NOTHING is guaranteed!

Sometimes, the best that we can hope for is to first learn to truly love ourselves, as we already are, and then to love everyone else, as we have learned to love ourselves. Perhaps that is the greatest gift we can give, to ourselves and to others. After all, if we are all made in the image and likeness of God, as it tells us in Genesis 1:27, coming to a full recognition and appreciation of who we, and others, really are, is an awakening of the highest magnitude. And just maybe, as more and more of us awaken, the anguish felt by those cycling through failure, weakness, illness, abandonment, fear and ignorance could be better buffered and utilized for transformative awakening of society as a whole instead of as a soul-crushing sense of defeat and hopelessness.

When any one of us falls, we all fall. But, when any one of us awakens, we all awaken. We are all connected to one another, whether we recognize it yet or not. If you find yourself on the left-hand side of this equation, know that you are not alone AND that there is *always* the light of dawn after the dark night. If you are fortunate enough to find yourself on the right-hand side of this equation, give thanks for your abundance AND look for others to share it with. As always, Always Believe In Your Dreams!!!

Chapter 14

Roadblocks To Success

When people think of Iowa, they typically think of cornfields and miles upon miles of flat land. Davenport, Iowa, where I attended chiropractic school, however, is actually quite hilly in places, particularly where it rises to the west of the mighty Mississippi River. And, Palmer College of Chiropractic sits atop the steepest hill in town, Brady Street hill.

One day, while walking to my classes, I encountered a group of fellow students who had all gathered to watch an old Excalibur car that was struggling to make the grade. Now, if you've never seen one of these cars before, they look remarkably similar to the car from the movie <u>Chitty, Chitty, Bang, Bang</u>. So, naturally, I joined them in watching.

As the driver started to get more and more frustrated, various suggestions were offered up from those in my group. The first thing suggested by one of my fellow students was that salt should be applied to the roadway to afford the driver better traction. Even though it was the middle of July, everyone felt that the memory of the recent long, harsh winter should be addressed and dealt with before moving forward. Salt was liberally applied around the tires of the old Excalibur, but it did not do any good.

The next thing that was suggested was that the driver should press harder on the gas pedal. Everybody remembered the story of <u>The Little Engine That Could</u> and maybe the driver just wasn't trying hard enough! The driver pressed harder on the gas pedal and the old Excalibur made lots of noise and smoke. Everyone cheered at the increased effort, but still, no progress was made up the hill.

Another astute student suggested that the driver should back all the way down Brady Street hill to the very bottom, empty out all of his belongings and place any other unnecessary weight such as the car's doors, trunk lid and spare tire out onto the ground and then get a running start up the hill. Unfortunately, when the frazzled driver did this, he did not even make it half way as far up the hill as before.

About this time, a passing professional-looking, business-suit-wearing gentleman stated that the driver was in the wrong type of car for making such a climb in the first place. He advised the driver to "grow up and drive something more respectable."

A nearby local minister, hearing the commotion, approached and counseled the driver that, according to his Book, it was sinful to want to make such a climb in the first place!

Fortunately, before the driver could change cars or give up his climb altogether, a rather quiet student stepped up to the old Excalibur and its rattled occupant and stated the following: "Clear the salt from the roadway and leave it be. Ease up on the gas pedal and cease your struggling. Gather ALL of your belongings and the dismantled parts of your car and put them back where they belong. Keep the beautiful car you have and prepare to continue your climb; but first, *take your other foot off of the brake!!!*" The driver did as instructed and completed his climb without any further difficulty.

Most of us go through life with one foot on the brake at all times. We create our own struggles and get in our own way. We never accomplish all that we are capable of. Like the student who suggested adding salt to the roadway in the middle of July, we get caught up re-living and resuscitating our past problems and perceived failures instead of just moving forward. Or, just like pressing harder and harder on the gas pedal, we become addicted to struggle, constantly trying harder and harder at strategies that don't work for us. Sometimes, we opt for short-term solutions to long-term problems. Dumping everything and starting over fresh, whether in the form of bankruptcy, change of job, change of partner or change of geographic location typically leaves us with less than where we originated from, much like our driver who backed down the hill, dumped any "excess weight" and tried for a running start. As long as we continue to keep our other foot on the brake, however, it is all for naught.

Pressures for conformity are ever present through our colleagues, co-workers, neighbors and even strangers. Staying true to ourselves requires a never ending vigilance. And then, there are those feelings of unworthiness that can block us from ever accepting our good, no matter what form it shows up in. In each and every one of these instances, however, the only one blocking us from our dreams is us!

*As published in The Meadville Tribune's quarterly Active for Life supplement:

- **Success**
  [originally published in The Meadville Tribune and titled "Taking Action toward a better, healthier, more abundant you?" 10/27/2009]

- **Finding Your Purpose, Getting A Life**
  [originally published in The Meadville Tribune's Active for Life supplement as a 2-part article titled "Finding your purpose: Getting a Life" which ran 1/30/2010 & 4/28/2010]

- **Things Cost Too Much**
  [originally published in The Meadville Tribune's Active for Life supplement as a 2-part article titled: "Things cost too much!...and other thoughts holding you back" which ran 7/30/2010 and titled: "Visualization a powerful tool to defeat negative thoughts" which ran 10/27/2010]

- **Soulmates**
  [originally published in The Meadville Tribune's Active for Life supplement and

titled: "Steps to avoid looming loneliness of retirement." Which ran 1/29/2011]

- **Say Thank You And Get Well Sooner**
  [originally published in The Meadville Tribune's Health & Science section and titled: "Thank you! Healing power of positive emotions." which ran 2/22/2011]

- **Living A Life With No Regrets**
  [originally published in The Meadville Tribune's Active for Life supplement and titled the same, which ran 4/27/2011]

- **Transcendental Living: Journeys Of A Lifetime**
  [originally published in The Meadville Tribune's Active for Life supplement and titled the same, which ran 7/30/2011]

- **What's Your Story?**
  [originally published in The Meadville Tribune's Active for Life supplement and titled: "What's your story? Why do you get up in the morning?" which ran 10/26/2011]

- **Soulmates II**
  [originally published in The Meadville Tribune's Active for Life supplement and

titled: "Soulmates II: The topic of love at any age." Which ran 1/29/2012]

- **Finding Your Afflatus**
  [originally published in The Meadville Tribune's Active for Life supplement and titled: "Have you found your afflatus yet?" which ran 4/25/2012]

- **Finding Inner Peace Without Caving To Outside Noise**
  [originally published in The Meadville Tribune's Active for Life supplement and titled the same, which ran 7/29/2012]

- **How The Coming Election Will Change Your Finances**
  [originally published in The Meadville Tribune's Active for Life supplement and titled the same, which ran 10/31/2012]

- **Awakening Through Change**
  [originally published in The Meadville Tribune's Active for Life supplement and titled: "You are the master of a better world." Which ran 4/25/2013]

- **Roadblocks To Success**
  [originally published in The Meadville Tribune's Active for Life supplement which ran in 2013]

Section II

The Blogs

Ask Me Who I Was

[the following article came about following a discussion with my son, a high school senior, after he came down with a mild case of "senioritis"]

Senioritis... Deal With It Now BEFORE It's Too Late!

As the 1st Quarter of the school year draws nigh, it is highly likely that most, if not all, of you are feeling the effects of the plague commonly referred to as "senioritis." After 12 LONG years of disciplined schooling, and with graduation visible on the near horizon, it is normal to reflect back on your education thus far in an attempt to make sense of it all. In many respects, you may feel that there have been way too many senseless, stupid rules to follow. And certainly, academia's emphasis on punishment for non-performance can leave you feeling discouraged and even bitter at times. Add in the sense of overwhelm brought on by schedule overload via extra-curricular activities, part-time jobs, family obligations and so-on and many of you are likely to be left feeling that you just don't care any more. After all, mandated schooling, with all of its rules, requirements and possible punishments is just about over. Then, you can finally get on with the business of actually living your lives, right? In the meantime, what's the harm in only doing the bare minimum requirements? Coasting feels good, doesn't it?

Motivational speaker and author T. Harv Eker states, "How you do **anything** is how you do **everything**."(1) By allowing the plague of "senioritis" to infect your thinking, you are setting yourselves up to lead lives of struggle and lack. Believe it or not, high school is a microcosm for life. Once you graduate, you are still going to have to deal with people you don't like, "senseless" rules and duties you don't agree with and busy schedules that overwhelm. Only then, the punishment system for non-performance is far harsher. What happens when you are 23 years of age and you get fired from your job because of your bad attitude; meanwhile you or your girlfriend/wife is pregnant and you are a month behind on the rent or mortgage? Talk about punishment for non-performance!

Doing the bare minimum and not caring is living life at the lowest rung on the ladder of personal development. After high school, the responsibilities (family, career, cost of living) and potential punishments (getting fired or passed over for promotion, homelessness, losing children to protective services, prison) grow exponentially. And yet, if you would merely focus on being all you can be **right now**, doing your best in any and every situation for your own personal development, any potential punishments for non-performance would be a non-issue and you would easily rise to the top of whatever field you chose, living at the top of the personal development ladder.

You are all welcome, and encouraged, to grow up and develop a better plan of your own to bring back and implement. However, in the meantime, you have to deal **now** with how it currently is. Focus on being the best you possible! Every choice you make has consequences now and in the future. Excellence is nothing more than the habit, consistently applied, of **always** doing your best.

Robert Frost writes in his poem <u>The Road Not Taken</u>, "Two roads diverged in a wood, and I, I took the one less traveled by, and that has made all the difference."(2) Those two roads are "senioritis," no longer caring vs. doing your best always and applying yourself in spite of seemingly stupid rules and punishments. Your senior year should be filled with hope and dreams for a brighter tomorrow. For the first time in your lives you are approaching that summit that actually enables you to plan out your future. Up until now, most of your schedules have been dictated to you by your parents, teachers, guidance counselors and coaches. That is all about to change. You are about to have the biggest say you have ever had in the direction of your life. What will you do with it? Defer it to someone else or rise to the occasion and actually become who you have always longed to be? Who you choose to be today sets the standard for who you will become tomorrow. Choose wisely!

Where Does Compassion Fit In Your Approach?

I recently posed the following question to one of the top motivational speakers in the country:

"Where does compassion fit in your approach? Or do you subscribe to the law of attraction viewpoint that suggests that everyone who falls on hard times has somehow attracted his or her circumstance? And, if so, how would you explain the Holocaust, for example?"

While they did not respond, someone else did weigh in with the following question:

"My question to you @Dr. Jon M. Ketcham would be do you believe that anything remotely close to the Holocaust could happen again to the people affected? If the answer is no I would suggest that THOSE PEOPLE (emphasis added) are attracting something different today. - Just a thought."

Here is my reply:

"In response to your question, i do not believe that anyone who was impacted by the Holocaust ever "attracted" it in the first place. This whole "Law of Attraction" thing is nothing more than a propagandized approach to feeling good about ourselves and our selfish whims while completely divorcing ourselves from the plight of others. There is not a shred of evidence showing similar behavior, like attracting like, anywhere in nature: not in physics, not in chemistry and not in biology; quite the opposite actually. And, most religious and spiritual texts do not support it either. The Law of Attraction promotes judgment and intolerance under the guise of empathy (awareness of the plight of others so you do not attract similarly) yet is totally devoid of compassion (giving a shit about the plight of others). Do i think a Holocaust-like event could ever take place again? Absolutely! As long as we perpetuate this divisive, we/them mentality, ALL people are at risk. It is likely to occur again and again, over time, for a whole host of seemingly justifiable reasons."

I share this for the following reason: for as long as any of us can separate out any segment of the population as "those people" we are all very much at risk.

Re-thinking Jesus: Spiritual Food for Thought.

Why did Jesus hang out primarily with the broken? Prostitutes, convicts, homeless and poor people were the ones he spent the majority of his time with. Conventional wisdom and Christian tradition throughout the millennia have suggested that Jesus 'ministered' to those most in need of saving.

However, much like how, in times of war, history is interpreted and written by the victors, what if the above referenced viewpoint is merely the outside-in interpretation of the survivors, spectators and general population, from that time period as well? If you do not think this happens, just ask the Native Americans who the real savages were during the settling of America. It may be called blasphemous but what if, just once, we used our God-given ability to think for ourselves rather than just accepting carte blanche the interpretations of others passed down throughout the ages?

What if Jesus hung out with the broken because, being spiritually awakened to loving compassion himself, or what some might call enlightened, he was most likely to 'get' them, in spite of their current situation AND, being broken, they were most likely to be enlightened themselves, because of their current situation, and thus, able to 'get' him as well? Let's be honest here, in Jesus time period, if anyone was truly in need of saving, it was the religious and political leaders, the Pharisees, much more so than those he chose to hang out with. The religious and political leaders would also have given him much more bang for his buck, so to speak, in terms of mass influence at the time. Maybe Jesus did not 'minister' so much as 'flock' with like-minded souls. Maybe we have gotten him wrong all these centuries?

The 2 Truths Every Expert, Guru, Influencer, Speaker, Coach, Consultant & Mentor Know But Won't Likely Tell You (but probably should!):

1.) **I am not an expert.** (and neither is anyone else who claims to be!)
In fact, the more I learn about EVERYTHING, the less, I come to realize, I know about ANYTHING. The only thing I can ever truly profess to be an expert on is my own life. I am free to interpret and give meaning to my own life experiences, but even that is highly subjective and, therefore, debatable. Any help I offer you is going to be based, at best, upon my own life experiences, which may or may not work for your particular circumstances.

2.) **You don't actually need my help.** (or anyone else's either!)
Suggesting otherwise robs you of your innate connection to Divinity. You could figure out the answers to everything that you are seeking on your own. You already have everything you think you need within your own reach, within yourself, if only you could silence the outside noise of life and listen to the wee small voice

within. All any expert can ever hope to accomplish, at best, is to re-kindle your inner fire and re-connect you with your own inner guidance.

Caught in the Storm of the "I"

What is the storm of the "I"?

Put simply, the storm of the "I" is our battle for identity and the ensuing struggle to hang on to it in times of adversity.

It's human nature to compare ourselves to others. We want to live lives that matter. We want to be part of something bigger than ourselves. Then, along comes an event that makes us question our identity or, sometimes, strips us of it entirely. In the movie, <u>The Boy in the Striped Pajamas</u>, after suffering a nasty fall, young Bruno encounters Pavel, a "farmer" who works in the kitchen and "gave up being a doctor" to "peel potatoes", unaware that Pavel is actually a prisoner of the adjacent concentration camp during the time of the Holocaust.

What happens when the labels, identities and titles we identify ourselves by get completely erased?

Our ego-driven self is small-minded, fearful and constraining. It wants to force-fit everyone, ourselves included, into narrowly defined, little identity boxes. Taking on the constipated views it has self-created, as well as those put on us by others, it seeks to forge a veritable identity-lock on who we are and who we can become. During times of identity loss, our EGO goes kicking and screaming into the Dark Night of the Soul. Some equate the intense pain of shedding our EGO with the process of reaching toward enlightenment.

In the **Bible,** according to the **Book of Luke, Chapter 17, Verse 21,** *The kingdom of God is within you.* **Psalm 23** states: *I shalt not want...my cup runneth over.* Similarly, in the **Bhagavad Gita,** according to the **Eighteenth Teaching, verse 61,** Lord Krishna states, *The lord resides in the heart of all creatures.* In the **Eighteenth Teaching, verse 78,** Sanjaya continues, *Where Krishna is...there do fortune, victory, abundance...exist.* And, according to **Tibetan Buddhist precepts,** *the secret wisdom of the Dzogchen teaches us that whatever we are looking for, it is always right here...what we seek, we already are.*

Numerous highly revered, sacred, spiritual teachings, like those listed above, remind us that our true self is actually limitless and Divine. There is nothing bigger than our true self. It cannot be contained or constrained, it just is.

Martial arts legend, Bruce Lee, famously said, *Empty your mind. Be formless and shapeless, like water. Don't think...FEEL!* In the battle for conformity versus being your true self, rather than caving to the screaming EGO, listen carefully for the all-powerful whispers of your soul. In other words, learn to be without your identities, labels and titles. Learn to just BE!

Ask Me Who I Was

Starting Over – Anyone, NOT Everyone, Can Do Anything

In the Pixar film, Ratatouille, there is an underlying theme of "anyone can cook," based upon famous chef Auguste Gusteau's best- selling book with the same title. This does not mean that everyone can cook, only that the gift of culinary art can come through anyone, regardless of background, or in this particular film's case, species.

Not everyone is meant, or gets, to do everything they want to do. In fact, not everyone gets to do anything they want to do.

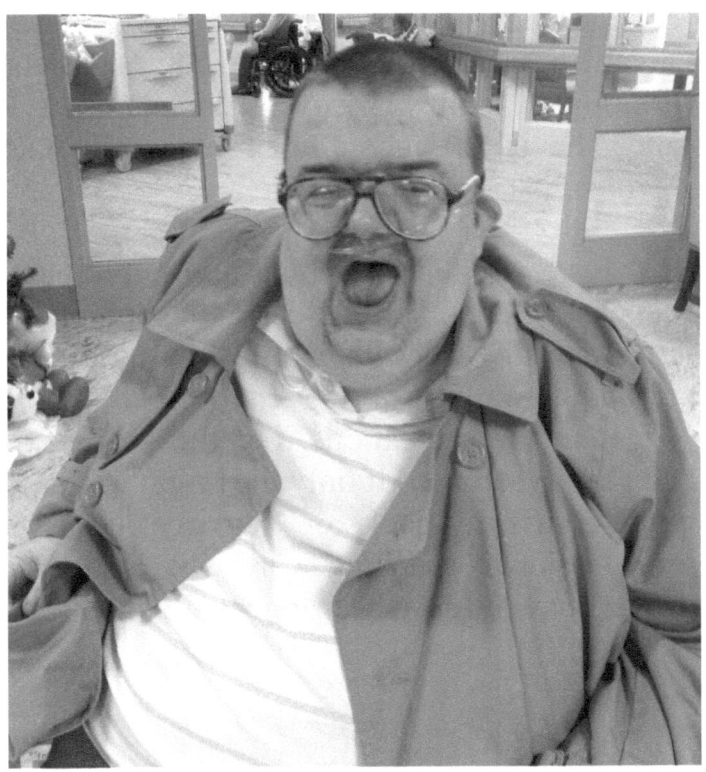

The beautiful human being pictured above is my brother Michael. Mike's wants are probably not all that different from your own. He yearns for mobility - the ability to self-determine; earning power – the ability to contribute while pursuing his passions; and romance – reciprocal love and connection. You see, more than anything else in the world, Mike wants to be able to drive a car, so he can take trips; he wants to open and run his own beauty shop; and Mike wants to find a girlfriend, preferably one with a car (LOL), and someday get married. Unfortunately for Mike, he suffered complications at birth and was born with profound, severe mental retardation and is physically handicapped as well. He lived at home until our mother passed away and I left for college. Since then, for the past 34 years, Michael has lived in a variety of nursing homes. Michael is never going to realize any of his dreams. Now, in his instance, he is not mentally or physically capable. But, what about those of us who are?

I have worked at writing and public speaking for the past 7 years, writing, designing and publishing 3 books; crafting, rehearsing and filming 2 complete talks; and literally working every spare minute to then market these creations. For the longest time, I convinced myself that, if only the "right" person were to come across my books or view my online videos, my professional speaking career would take off. However, having now been rejected as a speaker 14 times by TEDx events and 4 times by TED, over the past 3 years, all across the United States and in Canada as well, it has finally dawned on me that maybe there is no "right" person out there. As one of my more blunt TEDx rejection letters stated (the only one not a form-letter rejection actually), perhaps my talks are just "not a fit" anywhere.

If you have the mental and physical capacity to follow your dreams, I HIGHLY RECOMMEND that you do so. You will never know what you are capable of unless you try. And, by "try," I mean go all out with 100% effort, no excuses. Just don't beat yourself up if you don't get your hearts desire every time. As I state in my 1st talk video, "Failure Talks":

If you fail to realize your afflatus,
If your dreams do not come true,
You can always dream another dream,
You can always start anew.

Here's to all of you who, like me, find yourself starting over anew once more.

Ask Me Who I Was

Mike's Obituary

Mike was the perpetual child, retarded to the level of a 7 year old for most of his life. In spite of our parents', and, later, my, constant admonitions to not talk to strangers, Mike talked to EVERYONE, asking them to come see him sometime, for some pop money and to take him for rides. And, because he was so incredibly charming, he often got his wish. To know Mike was to love him. He was most in his glory with a fresh pack of paper and a new assortment of colored pens. Throw in a little money for the pop machine and Mike was a friend for life!

As my role transformed from one of younger sibling, sitting eagerly on his lap as he delightedly read to me, to one of guardian, overseeing all of his needs these past 20 years, Mike taught me many things:
- PATIENCE: never tiring of my perpetual delays of most of what he wanted to do.
- HOPE: Someday, maybe he would get to drive a car, find a girlfriend with a car, start his own beauty shop and take long trips to faraway zoos.
- LOVE: Mike was the litmus test by whom I chose my wife. As my wife, Lisa, will tell you, I waited to propose to her until AFTER she met Mike. Anyone who couldn't accept Mike

and the HUGE part he was, and would always be, of my life was not even an option to me.
- FORGIVENESS: Mike, to my knowledge, NEVER uttered a swear word and never held a grudge against anyone for anything. He was just as glad to hear from someone who had not spoken to him in decades as he was to speak to me, maybe more so.

I am who I am today, in no small measure, thanks to knowing, loving and being loved by Mike. The void left by Mike's passing is beyond words.

False Prophets, Ostriches & Groupies – The Delusions of Social Media and its Messiahs

Who are you "connected" to on LinkedIn? How many Facebook "friends" and "followers" do you have? We live in a world where we've been conditioned to measure our self-worth by how many digital connections and interactions we accumulate, by how many views and "likes" our posts receive. How do you stack up?

How many of your "connections" and "friends" have ever actually been there for you? Recommended you to others? Assisted you on your journey without asking anything of you in return? How many of them have you done likewise for? How many of them even know, or care, that you exist? And, if they don't, why are you "connected" to or "friends" with them at all?!?

Many are content merely to be associated with those they perceive as having reached a certain level of greatness: perhaps, by a touch of His cloak, they'll be healed. Self-proclaimed prophets and gurus regularly churn out new "content" for their adoring fans, followers and groupies. This fosters and perpetuates an inherent inequality, a "we / them" mentality, discriminating between messiahs and followers, superiority and inferiority, worthy and unworthy. In far too many instances, gurus and followers alike bury their heads in the sand, like the proverbial ostrich, to any who might oppose their views, to any who can bring them no immediate gain.

We live at a point in electronic history where events like TED and TEDx talks, approximately 50,000 talks designed to bring the best innovations in technology, education and design to the forefront, are currently available worldwide on YouTube, with over one billion views to date. And yet, are we really any better off because of it? **What has happened to our humanity?** According to a recent United Nations report on extreme poverty and human rights, Philip Alston writes, "The United States is one of the world's richest, most powerful and technologically innovative countries, but neither its wealth nor its power nor its technology is being harnessed to address the situation in which 40 million people continue to live in poverty." (1)

In The Diary of a Young Girl, Anne Frank says, *"Despite everything, I believe that people are really good at heart."* (2) This was certainly not the reality of the times during which young Anne wrote. It also was definitely not the reality of her final days as "neighbors" ultimately betrayed her family and led to her being sent to slaughter. And yet, perhaps, just maybe her sentiment, the sentiment of a young, naïve, horribly deluded teenager, has led to a kinder, gentler planet as people all over the world have been transformed by her world views; as people strive to live up to her innocent enough expectations.

In a world where everyone's sole value has been seemingly reduced down to what they can provide someone with, seeing everyone as either a prospective customer, client, fan or follower, I find myself hoping with all of my being that young Anne Frank was right.

Ask Me Who I Was

Dodging the Most Useless Question in the World – How to Stop Languishing & Start Living Again

We have to have something to hold onto to believe in.
Erica [Quarrel short-film] (1)

History gets written, and subsequently interpreted, by the victors or, at the very least, by the survivors, in any given time period, making its irrefutable authenticity suspect at best. As a species, humans are "meaning makers," constantly aggregating into collective societies who ascribe to their self-imposed like meanings and crucifying, stoning and burning at the stake any who do not "believe" their particular spin on things. Everywhere you turn, people are "interpreting" events and circumstances they find themselves in as the will of their particular deity, the result of their personal and collective efforts or the consequences of some inadequacy or infraction.

We are prone to constantly reviewing our past events, attaching endless meanings to them, in a desperate attempt to make sense of our present and, hopefully, to somehow then successfully predict our futures. However, as Robert Burns' poem, To a Mouse, reminds us, "the best laid plans of mice and men often go awry." (2) In times like that, in the midst of loss, perhaps the most useless question in the world one can ask themselves is: "Why me?!?"

There is an infinite list of possible answers to that particular question. Then again, there might not be an answer short of "just because." Truth of the matter is, no matter which answer you pick, it doesn't, it cannot, change what has already occurred and, worse, it distracts you from taking appropriate action now. Whatever has passed has passed! Regardless of how you decide to interpret it, it can never be altered. Your only real power to influence any change whatsoever exists in the now.

It's helpful, at times, to know where you have been; but, it's infinitely more important, at all times, to know where you are actively going. Imagine that you are piloting a boat on a long voyage when, suddenly, you encounter turbulent waters. Finding the cause of the unexpected turbulence might be helpful for future journeys, but initially, all that matters right away is how you are going to steer your boat clear of the current turbulence. Don't let yourself become so enamored with the past that you miss out, maniacally attempting to unwrap the mysterious past and missing out entirely on the exposed present. Instead of belaboring "Why me?!?", try asking yourself instead, "Now what?" What are you going to do next? How shall you respond now?

Section III

The Talks

Ask Me Who I Was

Failure Talks

TED is a non-profit organization devoted to *"Ideas Worth Spreading"* where speakers are asked to give the talk of their lives in 18 minutes or less.

My attempts to make sense of my own insignificant life and my audacity in thinking that my experiences might be worthy of sharing with others are what gave rise to this talk, written in accordance with the TED format. Rejected more than a dozen times by numerous, independent TEDx and TED events, across the United States and Canada, over a 3 year period, it remains the talk of my lifetime nonetheless.

You can watch portions of this talk on YouTube at: **https://youtu.be/5zznWSvJ9PQ**

Ask Me Who I Was

Failure Talks – A Dual Entendre – Rising from the Ashes to Dream Another Dream

I once heard a motivational speaker lament, "What a shame it is that FAILURES don't give talks, because there's so much you could learn from them if they did."

6 years ago, I was living the dream! I had a waiting-list chiropractic practice, earning over $100,000/year, while working only part-time hours. I had just published my very first book and was getting ready to write my second... I thought my future was **unstoppable***! Then,... the insurance industry* **completely** *rewrote all the rules. Literally overnight, my practice was* **decimated***. My income quickly dwindled to less than 10% of what it had been. I spent the next* **16 months** *desperately looking for other work, as I frantically struggled to avoid the inevitable foreclosures and tax sales. Finally, after sending out more than 80 resumes, only three of which ever turned in to interviews, and contacting more than 50 publishers with my 2nd book,* **none of whom** *had any interest in it whatsoever, I found work in a completely different field...***accounting***, now working twice as many hours for less than half the pay my family had grown accustomed to. Nearly 25 years worth of intensive study, blood, sweat and tears* *dedicated to my chiropractic career were completely flushed away!*

- *All the rules had all changed and I... I had failed to adapt.*

[SLIDE I]

And yet, in losing everything, I received a gift quite unlike any other, perhaps the 2nd greatest gift I have ever been given.

Our *ability to hope and dream is instilled in us at birth and represents our connection to our Source / to God / the Universe*
Your *hopes and dreams give DIRECTION, MEANING & PURPOSE to your life. They are your* **raison d'etre***; your reason for being; sometimes referred to as your Divine Design, your Primary Purpose and your Life Mission.*
Author Paulo Coehlo calls it your Personal Legend. Pixar's Wall-E calls it your Prime Directive.
The Roman philosophers and poets: Cicero, Horace & Virgil, referred to it as your **AFFLATUS***, literally, your inspiration* **direct** *from the breath of GOD!*

[SLIDE II]

*Sometimes, when we follow our afflatus, and pursue our dreams, things go **smoothly**...oftentimes, they do not!. Life can be a very fickle & formidable mistress.*

*In the Bible, after Job loses EVERYTHING of value to him: his health, his wealth, his reputation... even his family, he **cries out**, "...**and I am reduced to dust and ashes**," where dust and ashes were symbolic of great humiliation and insignificance, a process I've come to know as the zero's journey.*

[SLIDE III]

*When all was said and done, the casualties from my personal zero's journey were very high: my identities as a doctor, business owner, provider for my family and contributor to my community were completely erased. My prestige for having graduated in the top 5% of my class at Chiropractic school, a class of more than 230 students that had been deemed "the most academically astute class to come down the pike in many years" was rendered completely meaningless. I lost my chosen livelihood and my cherished lifestyle. I lost all of my wealth and most of my wealth-making capability. But, the biggest loss I suffered, **by far**, was the colossal loss of time available to spend together with the love of my life, my wife Lisa.*

Ask Me Who I Was

[SLIDES IV & V]

Meeting Lisa was the greatest gift I've ever been given. Lisa and I did EVERYTHING together: she was by my side throughout Chiropractic school and then the office manager for my now failed practice, we parented together, shopped together. We even shared a single vehicle for most of our 27 years together. And, while some might consider the amount of time we once shared excessive, neither of us could have imagined, or desired, life any other way.
Lisa ultimately found work as the office manager for a busy medical practice, 12 months to the day before I found my position in accounting, forcing her to work LONG 10-12 hour days apart from me in order to earn in a day what I was once capable of generating for us in under an hours time.

People who have suffered the amputation of a limb commonly report experiencing what are known as "phantom" limb pains, where they experience extreme pain in the area just BEYOND where the amputation took place... as though the severed limb were still attached to their body, even though it is gone. I can only begin to describe the very real physical, emotional and spiritual pain that I felt, following this drastic reduction in time with Lisa, as being akin to phantom limb pain. I could still feel her presence, as though she was still by my side, but she was nowhere to be found.

[SLIDE VI (black)]

Any further attempts to put into words the indescribable pain and anguish that this forced separation caused to my soul would be impossible to meaningfully convey. Suffice it to say that I wished very earnestly, on more than one occasion, to be "returned to sender" so-to-speak. At least if I would have died, through the prospect of life insurance proceeds, I would have once again been able to provide for the needs of my family.

Lao Tzu, Chinese philosopher and founder of Taoism states, *"When I let go of what I am, I become what I might be."*

I believe he is talking here about our attachments, our outward clinging of the spirit, as Saint John of the Cross called it back in 1578.

Saint John of the Cross *viewed, what he called the Dark Night of the Soul, as a gift from God designed specifically to free us from our* **attachments***.*

Meister Eckhart – German theologian& mystic – who lived 300 years prior to Saint John of the Cross *believed that the only function of hell was to burn away the part of you that won't let go of your* *life, your attachments. He saw it as a means of freeing your soul.*

Tibetan Buddhism *teaches that our attachments are one of the primary causes of all suffering, referring to them as **poisons** or **fires**.*

For me, while it felt like dying while still alive, the GIFT I found contained in walking the Zero's Journey is exactly the same one each of these authors have spoken of. *Our **attachments** to our accomplishments; to our identities, labels and titles; to outcomes, people and things limit and imprison our souls. When we let go of our rigidly held limited ideas about who we think we are, we start to see far more similarities than differences among us all.*

*Out of **great humiliation and insignificance**, the seeds of loving compassion can **take root** and bloom. Perhaps, through the kindness extended by a stranger, hope can reemerge. The Calvary may not have come, with bugles blaring, to save the day; but I've found that a gentle touch, a warm smile, a non-judgmental acceptance and reassurance can be life-saving to someone. The phoenix that arises from the ashes of loss, suffering, humiliation and despair is one that **readily recognizes** the suffering of others and is no longer capable of sitting idly by in indifference.*

*When it comes right down to it, we are **ALL** alone. Most of what happens to us happens by chance. The best way to improve **our** chances is by actively working to improve the chances for someone else. If you want to have **your** prayers answered, start helping answer the prayers of others. If each of us did this for one another, perhaps, one day, ALL of our prayers might actually get answered too. The Golden Rule tells us to treat others as we would like others to treat us. This is the **Golden Role** each of us must play in the lives of one another.*

Aristotle believed in a process he called **ENTELECHY**

[SLIDE VII]

*Life wants, **NO**, Life **demands** that you follow your afflatus & pursue your dreams so you can become who you were meant to be.*
Whether you actually succeed or not is irrelevant. Their real value comes as a result of who they nudge you to become while in their pursuit: a human "becoming", awakened to loving compassion for yourself AND one another. And who you become can NEVER be taken away from you [unless you voluntarily surrender it by giving up on life].

If you fail to realize your afflatus, if your dreams do not come true, you can always dream another dream, you can always start anew.

And, just maybe, perhaps broken dreams provide some of the best fertilizer to the seeds of loving compassion lying dormant in each and every one of us.

When you leave here tonight, go out and find 3 people currently lost on their own zero's journey like I was, people living with broken dreams, suffering in silence, crying themselves to sleep at night, all alone, wondering if it is even worthwhile to go on living. You won't have to go very far to find them. They are your friends and family members, your neighbors and co-workers. That stranger you pass by every day on your way to and from work. Whoever they are, go seek them out.

Don't judge them or the circumstances you find them in. *As my wife put it so eloquently, "True compassion is understanding that Darkness is*

Darkness and not judging the circumstances that turned out the light."

1. ***simply love them***
2. ***let them know they are NOT alone***
3. ***assure them, "it's going to be OK;" TELL THEM <u>THEY</u> are going to be OK.***

Without your love AND encouragement, they might never be inspired to dream another dream, to start anew.

What a tragic loss that would be... for all of us. Our dreams are not just for us. They are given to each of us for the benefit of **all of us**, for the betterment of humanity.

And, if YOU currently find yourself in the midst of your own zero's journey, I want you to know:

1. *You ARE loved. I love you!*
2. *You're NOT alone! I know what it's like to follow a dream, to give it your all, and still come up short anyways, time and time and time again.* "This talk is a prime example. Over the past 3 of years, I have applied to speak it 18 different times at various TEDx and TED events, all across the country, and in Canada too, only to be rejected each and every single time. If I can still dream another dream, if I can start anew, you can too!

3. *It's going to be OK. YOU are going to be OK.*

Now, let's go dream another dream!

audacious brain farts

Ask Me Who I Was

Perversion, Sin & Death

Blaspheming the "law of attraction":
- Unsupported by science
- Counter to numerous Sacred, spiritual teachings including:
    - The Holy Bible
    - The Bhagavad-Gita
    - Tibetan Buddhism
- And potentially deadly!

In the words of Nietzsche, *"Sometimes, people don't want to hear the truth because they don't want their illusion destroyed."*

Also written in accordance with the TED format, and also rejected numerous times by independent TEDx and TED events across the United States, over a 3 year period.

You can watch this talk on YouTube at: **https://youtu.be/e3m8PvEXrh0**

Ask Me Who I Was

Perversion, Sin & Death: The *Dirty* Little Secret That Broke the Law of Attraction

If you repeat a fairy tale often enough, and with enough conviction, it starts to look and feel like an apparent truth to the masses, even though it is still false.

- *[PAUSE]*
- *Everyone <u>knows</u> that like attracts like.*
- *[PAUSE]*

When you Google "Law of Attraction", it brings up more than 16 million results! The LoA 1st gained notoriety through the New Thought movement during the late 1800s. Its defining Core belief is that: **like attracts like**

- Like Thoughts…
- Like Feelings/Emotions…
- Like Actions…
- …All go out into the ethers and **somehow** magnetize similar back unto themselves.

2° to this 1° belief is a belief in the: **existence & prevalence of lack**. Hence, the "need" to attract in the 1st place.

- *[PAUSE]*

But, what if EVERYTHING the Law of Attraction is based upon is false? Not only false, but dangerous. Deadly, even!
- *[PAUSE]*

1.) Perversion of Law <u>(attraction vs reflection)</u>

Nowhere in the natural world does "like attract like." ...NOWHERE!

Take the world described by the laws of Physics, for example:

- ***With Magnets***
  - *Like poles repel one another while opposite poles attract.*
- ***With Electricity***
  - *Like and opposite charges behave similarly.*
- ***The laws of Biology, Chemistry & Physiology are much the same:***
  - *Solutes dissolved in solution diffuse from high concentrations to low concentrations [opposites moving toward each other] until a state of equilibrium is reached [likes, side by side] at which point nothing further occurs.*

Thus... suggesting the existence of a LoA, where like attracts like, is actually promoting a perversion of known natural laws!

2.5) Law of Reflection

*Maybe it's not about what you are "attracting" to you. What if it's more about what you are 1st putting out there that ultimately gets **reflected** back to you? Like may not attract like, but like DOES reflect like!*

Think of a smile. If you go out into the world trying to "attract" a smile, all the while frowning [grimace], you won't likely see very many smiles. In fact, you'll probably frighten people. But, if you go out and just smile, genuinely, at others, even if your teeth are not your own, many will smile back at you, reflecting your smile back to you from multiple directions.

2.75) LoA...LoR, What's the big deal?

*Now, at first glance, you might say to yourself, "LoA...LoR, what's the big deal anyways? It's just semantics, right? Aren't they saying the exact same thing?" Actually, not really, **<u>not even close!</u>***

Imagine shining a flashlight at a mirror in a darkened room. What gets reflected back to you is based solely upon the entirety of what you initially shone out or emitted. Your light was whole to begin with!

2.) Sin against Religious Law/Teaching <u>(lack vs wholeness)</u>

Numerous highly revered, sacred and spiritual teachings speak of our innate wholeness, in direct defiance to any suggestion of lack.

- In the **Bible**
  - According to the **Book of Luke, Chapter 17, Verse 21**
    - The kingdom of God is within you.
  - **Psalm 23** *states:*
    - *I shalt not want...my cup runneth over.*
- Similarly, in the **Bhagavad Gita,**
  - According to the **Eighteenth Teaching, verse 61,** Lord Krishna states,
    - The lord resides in the heart of all creatures.
  - In the **Eighteenth Teaching, verse 78,** Sanjaya continues,

- *Where Krishna is...there do fortune, victory, abundance...exist.*
- *And, according to **Tibetan Buddhist precepts,***
  - *The secret wisdom of the Dzogchen teaches us that whatever we are looking for, it is always right here...what we seek, we already are.*

Thus...because of its reliance upon the existence and prevalence of lack, the LoA is actually committing sin against numerous holy doctrines!

3.) Death (of Compassion/Humanity)

And yet, the LoA persists despite the preponderance of evidence to the contrary, spreading like a cancer throughout all facets of society.

As it has approached an almost cult-like fervor, it has devolved into a mainstream, propagandized approach for people to feel good about themselves and the pursuit of their own selfish whims, while completely divorcing themselves from the plight of others. It promotes judgment and intolerance under the guise of empathy, an awareness of the plight of others (so one does not attract similarly), yet it is totally devoid of compassion, actually caring about the plight of others. Labeling people as: failures, losers & low lifes; infidels, low resonators & non-believers; savages, sinners & terrorists, **enables empathy while simultaneously inoculating against compassion***: "they got what they deserve," "***they attracted it,***" making it ok for others to suffer because of their erroneous ancestry, heritage or race; for their faulty beliefs, orientation or actions;* **for not having a sincere enough pumpkin patch;** *for not conforming to a feather like the rest of the flock. Such mass hysteria fuels our flock-like instincts, triggering distrust, anger, blame, and condemnation of any who are seen as being of a different feather.*

4.25) Moving from How can I avoid? To How can I help.

So, how do we move from Judgment & intolerance ➔ *To making it better? ...From How can I avoid? To How can I help?*

4.5) Law of Reflection – part ii

*Johann Wolfgang von Goethe [****Gō' tuh****] says, "Treat a man as he is and he will remain as he is. Treat a man as he can and should be, and he will become as he can and should be." Perhaps this is the highest and noblest use of the Law of Reflection. Whatever we have emitted is mostly what gets reflected back to us. Likewise, we mostly reflect back* to others whatever they have emitted. However, we can override our "reflective" tendency by **intentionally choosing** to recognize the Divinity within others, even those not yet aware of it within themselves, and reflect that back to them instead! In doing so, by loving the unlovable, we offer them glimpses, maybe for the first time in their lives, we offer them glimpses of their own Divinity, their own true nature, and enable them to live in to it thus up-leveling all of humanity.

4.)   Climax

Those contaminated by the Law of Attraction live in a world populated and ruled by:
- **PERVERTED MAGNETS**
- **HOLY SINNERS**
- **& HARBINGERS OF DEATH.**

5.)   Conclusion

Now, imagine a world populated and ruled by practitioners of the Golden Rule instead; where people actually treat others as they themselves would like to be treated. I already know which world I would rather live in.
- *How about you?*

Ask Me Who I Was

Section IV

The Books

Ask Me Who I Was

The Golden Role – Just Be Nice!
(2016)

The phoenix that arises from the ashes of loss, suffering, humiliation and despair is one that readily recognizes the suffering of others and is no longer capable of sitting idly by in indifference.

Written as the companion guide and work book to The "Zero's Journey", and based upon the Universal concept of the "golden rule," The Golden Role represents the passionate attempt of one semi-enlightened man to awaken others to humanity's cry of desperation for loving compassion before it is too late to save us all.

The "Zero's Journey" –A Modern-day Survival Guide to Weathering Accidental Enlightenment
(2014)

Famed mythologist Joseph Campbell talks about the "hero's journey" as a blueprint for the unfoldment of following your bliss. Essentially, each and every one of us are likened to tribal warriors or explorers who depart on some journey, encounter obstacles and adversity, fight the big fight, conquer our demons and then return home to share all that we have learned with the rest of our tribe. Everybody cycles through varying stages and degrees of this journey throughout their lifetimes.

However, as Robert Burns poem, To a Mouse, reminds us, "The best laid plans of mice and men / Often go awry."

On this journey to "accidental enlightenment," it is common to experience the complete decimation of any pre-conceived notions, roles and identities you have grown accustomed to identifying yourselves by. During this traumatic destruction of your EGO, it can seem as though God is reducing your very existence to absolute zero. This is **the "Zero's Journey!"**

Anyone who has ever suffered a great loss, whether relational, financial, career, health, spiritual or otherwise, knows all to well the depths of despair and the anguish that arise in what Saint John of the Cross referred to as The Dark Night of the Soul. The Dark Night of the Soul is all about pain, suffering and loss. Yet, out of all that, from the ashes that used to be your life, hopefully, like the Greek mythological phoenix, you emerge as more than you were when you started.

A written, first person account from someone who's "been there, bled that."

iContractor1 – Constructing Your Perfect Life by Remodeling YOU from the Inside-Out!
(2012)

Written at a time when I was more aptly described as "cocksure and clueless," no doubt. My freshman writing attempt: a little rough around the edges, for sure, but powerful nonetheless.

A simple, 3-step process backed by hundreds of thousands of years of literature that could make all of your dreams come true once and for all.

Ask Me Who I Was

BONUS Chapter from iContractor1:

Mirrors, Windows, Doors & Light

> "Your outer world is simply a reflection of your inner world."
> T. Harv Eker (1)

Legend has it that Socrates could often be found sitting outside the gates of Athens where he could greet strangers. One day, a man came up to him and said, "I am thinking about moving to Athens. What are the people who live in Athens like?" Socrates replied, "I'd be glad to tell you. But, first tell me about the people where you are from." To this, the man went into a tirade, "Oh, they are just horrible. Nobody cares about anyone but themselves. No one will help another who is in need, yet they are always minding others business. They will rob you blind, if you let them. I am leaving only cold-hearted enemies behind." Socrates, in his infinite wisdom replied, "Well, you might as well continue your search elsewhere because you will find it the same way here." So, the sour man continued elsewhere on his journey.

Some time later, another traveler casually approached Socrates and asked, "I am considering moving to Athens. Can you tell me a little about the people who live there?" Socrates again replied, "I'd be glad to. But first, tell me about the people where you are from." This time, the second traveler smiled warmly and said, "The people of my village are wonderful! Everybody looks out for their neighbor because, after all, we are all connected aren't we? We are all like family there. I am only traveling so I can expand my horizons and meet the neighbors and family members that I have yet to introduce myself to." Socrates smiled back and said, "Welcome to Athens brother. You will find the people here to be just like you have described."

> **"You don't get in life what you want.
> You get what you are."
> Les Brown (2)**

Why did Socrates embrace the second traveler while rejecting the first? Was it not possible that the two travelers came from very different types of cities? Or, did Socrates understand something far deeper than that? Perhaps he knew that other people could only reflect back to you your own beliefs about yourself and your environment. People merely mirror back to you who you were on the inside, based upon your prior thoughts and feelings or emotions. They can only reflect back to you what you have already put out there. Most likely Socrates knew that, in both situations, the traveler would find the city of Athens to be just like the places they came from. He knew that, wherever you go, there you are: thinking the same kinds of thoughts, feeling the same kinds of feelings or emotions and taking the same kinds of actions, thus causing the same kinds of situations to be reflected back unto yourself. Denying the first man entrance to the city of Athens was like preventing weeds from overtaking his garden.

> "Your dominant thoughts create your conditions."
> Napoleon Hill (3)

So, where do our thoughts and feelings come from? Contrary to popular belief, our thoughts and feelings do not exist solely as random, spontaneous reactions to our surroundings; at least they do not have to! In fact, we can actively choose to think and feel, or not think and feel, in certain ways. We can choose our response to any given circumstance. Viktor Frankl, a survivor of four WWII concentration camps of the Holocaust, wrote in <u>Man's Search For Meaning</u>, "Everything can be taken from a man but one thing: the last of the human freedoms – to choose one's attitude in any given set of circumstances, to choose one's own way." (4) In other words, no matter what happens to you, you can *always* choose your response, your thoughts and feelings. It is like the ancient Greek philosopher Epictetus stated, "Men are disturbed not by things, but by the views they take of them." (5)

Socrates asked the two travelers about their respective cities because he knew that our attitudes, our perceptions, our worldview are like windows through which we view our world. The condition of our windows colors our view and simultaneously announces it for all the world to know. Ralph Waldo Trine wrote in his masterpiece <u>In Tune With The Infinite</u>, back in 1897, "cease your complaining...keep your pessimism, your 'poor, unfortunate me' to yourself, lest you betray the fact that your windows are badly in need of something. But know that your friend, who keeps his windows clean, ...lives in a much different world from yours." (6) Our attitudes, perceptions and worldview serve as the windows through which we announce our current level of being to the world. Other people serve as mirrors, reflecting that state of being back to us.

> **"In my Father's house are many rooms."**
> **Bible (7)**

Ask any four year old what they want to do on any given day and their world is chock full of possibilities. Unfortunately, as we get older, our lives get busier and more scarred by disappointment, illness and loss. As such, we tend to see fewer and fewer opportunities around us. It can seem as though there are no open doors of opportunity left for us to enter.

The reality, however, is that opportunity is always around us, and it always has been. There are no fewer possibilities available to the adult than to the child. We just have to get back in touch with our inner child to see them. In fact, Joseph Campbell states, "When you follow your bliss, doors will open where you would not have thought there were going to be doors, and where there wouldn't be a door for anybody else." (8)

Even in the face of failure, there are always opportunities. Neale Donald Walsch, author of the Conversations With God series states, "All endings start something better. It is inevitable. When one door closes, another does open." (9) Just like Napoleon Hill stated back in 1937 in his classic Think And Grow Rich, "Every adversity, every failure and every heartache carries with it the seed of an equivalent or a greater benefit." (10) Problem is, we tend to get so wrapped up in our losses that we forget to look for the benefit(s) contained therein. That does not eliminate their existence however.

All of these doors of opportunity represent who you might become. But, unless you look for them and step through them, nothing changes. Everybody experiences loss and fear, but not everybody allows themselves to become paralyzed by it. Learning to Feel The Fear And Do It Anyway ®, as Susan Jeffers titled her wonderful book, can mean the difference between staying stuck versus growth and enjoyment. (11)

> **"When one door closes, another opens, but we often look so long and so regretfully upon the closed door that we fail to see the one that has opened for us."**
> **Alexander Graham Bell (12)**

Where we get mixed up is in thinking that these opportunities are, somehow, separate from us; on the other side of these doors, so to speak. Contrary to the opinions of the masses, the collective consciousness, we are not physical beings yearning for a spiritual connection. Rather, we are spiritual beings having a physical experience; an experience that often deceives us. Genesis 1:27 states, "God created man in His own image." (13) John 8:12 states, "I am the light of the world. He who follows Me shall not walk in darkness, but have the light of life." (14) John 10:30 continues, "I and My Father are one." (15) Separation from God is often described as "being in the dark." Survivors of near-death experiences all talk about going towards or returning to the light. When people figure out the solution to a long perplexing problem, they often say they have "seen the light." The truth is, we are all beings of light; light resonating with a dense vibrational form.

Putting it all together, we see that our attitudes and perceptions are the windows that color the light that emanates from within us. Others simply mirror back to us that which we have already emanated. And, the real clincher? Opportunity is not on the other side of the doors; it is within you already in the form of your innermost dreams. That is why we say that your dreams are INspired. Doors of opportunity do not open to reveal to you what is outside of you. Doors of opportunity open to let your light shine out! Your dreams are your gifts from God. Following those dreams is your gift to God.

"Launch yourself on every wave, find eternity in each moment."
Henry David Thoreau (16)

Denying your innermost longings is like closing your doors and putting a self-imposed prison upon your soul. Dr. John Demartini says, "The greatest cause of illness, disease and death is not living your dreams." (17) It will eat you from within.

We all use mirrors to check our appearance before going out in public, to make sure we look ok. We can use our metaphorical mirrors, other people and how they treat us, to check how we are doing in life. Do others generally treat us with respect, compassion and love? Or, does their behavior towards us suggest that we are not being all we can be? Perhaps the windows of our soul are in need of a good cleaning, streaked with the sludge of "aintitawfulism," pessimism, worry and fear. And what of our doors of opportunity? Are we able to recognize them in all of their bounteous splendor? Are we courageous enough to step through them when we do recognize them? Or, do we let self-doubt and prior loss paralyze us from taking action?

- **Mirrors – other people and how they treat us**
- **Windows – our thoughts (attitudes, perceptions & worldview)**
- **Doors – our innermost dreams**
- **Light – our true nature**

Motivational speaker and success guru Les Brown tells a wonderful story about a man who goes for a walk and passes by a house where people are gathered together around a porch. Along with them, the man sees and hears a dog whining and moaning in apparent pain. Curious, and rather concerned, the man approaches the gathering of people and asks, "What is wrong with that dog?" "That dog is laying on a nail that has protruded through the floorboard of the porch," he is told. "Then, why doesn't he get up and move to a different spot?" the man asks. "Because it doesn't hurt enough to make him move. It only hurts enough to make him complain," is their reply. (18) That protruding nail is your buried hopes and dreams, your many doorways of opportunity waiting to be opened. How bad does it have to get before you are spurred into action, not just complaint?!?

Far too many people die with their light still locked up inside them. They ignore their true needs and innermost longings because they fear what others will think of them; they fear the possibility of trying and failing; they feel unworthy and unable to afford what they truly desire. Leading lives of quiet desperation, their inner light dims until there is next to nothing! Every time you stifle your inner passions and deny yourself your dreams, a part of you dies. The time to pursue your dreams is NOW! When would NOW be a good time to start? If you are not growing, you are dying. Why not choose to stop dying? Stop denying your inner most longings. Listen to your heart. Fan that light back into a glorious flame. Follow your dreams and finally start to really live! Always Believe In Your Dreams!!!

Ask Me Who I Was

Section V

The Author

Ask Me Who I Was

Traditionally, this section is where authors toot their own horns, so to speak, building a resume of their many accomplishments and credentials while simultaneously giving you the readers a little sneak peek behind the curtains into their private lives as well. And, while I could build a sizable list here myself, truth be told, I could also build an equally impressive, probably even bigger, list of my many failures. It is easy to pat ourselves on the back when things are going well, but it is far harder to look at ourselves in the mirror with anything other than disdain when they are not.

Throughout this winding journey called life, particularly during times of stress and emotional upheaval, I have found writing to be helpful to me, so long as I don't let myself get too attached to the idea of anyone else wanting to actually read any of it. My 15 minutes of fame were over long before I ever even realized they had occurred at all. I continue to write nonetheless.

Ask Me Who I Was

About the Author

jon was in private practice as a chiropractor for 20 years and contributed a quarterly philosophy column to his hometown newspaper, The Meadville Tribune (circ. 12,000), in the Active for Life supplement, from 2009 until 2013. Prior to that, as part of a 10-year long collaborative effort by all of the local chiropractors, he contributed articles once or twice a year to The Meadville Tribune's monthly HealthBeat column. Additionally, he is the author of iContractor 1, which he published in 2012, The Zero's Journey, which he published in 2014, and The Golden Role, which he published in 2016.

When it comes right down to it, he is the first to acknowledge, "I am nobody; no better, no worse than anybody else. I am just doing the best I can with the resources I find before me, just like everybody else." In fact, rather than puffing out his chest and touting his credentials, he prefers to be addressed simply as "jon."

Much like Job from the Bible, jon has known more than his fair share of adversity and misfortune. Having gone broke 3X within 4 years, nearly dying from a life-threatening illness and skirting perilously close to homelessness, he immersed himself into a decade-long study of personal development and success that included reading over 100 classic works, repeatedly listening to more than two dozen audio programs and watching over a dozen videos. He was then able to turn his life around and build the "waiting-list" chiropractic practice of his dreams, only to have his entire livelihood completely evaporate following sweeping insurance company reductions in Pennsylvania in 2012 that took most of the fun and ALL of the viability out of private practice. By documenting his journey into hell and back, he leaves a trail of light to illuminate the way out for others still lost in the abyss of darkness, offering hope to the hopeless & helping the broken re-kindle their dreams, through his passionate books and talks.

jon lives with his wife in "wooded bliss" surrounded by 35 acres of dense forestland in Meadville, Pennsylvania. He has two beautiful, gifted children: a twenty-three-year-old son, who is a talented science fiction author / artist and budding film-maker and a twenty-year-old daughter, who is a pursuing a career in chemical engineering. He shares his home with ten cats, a bunny, a cockatiel, and chickens! All of his pets are "rescues."

jon's articles have been well received over the years and are also available by following his blogs at:

www.TheZerosJourney.com

audacious brain farts

and
www.AlwaysBelieveInYourDreams.com.

Ask Me Who I Was

Connecting to dr. ketcham

Websites:

AlwaysBelieveInYourDreams.com
- "Book the Doc" to speak at your next event!
- Follow "Doc's Blog"

TheZerosJourney.com
- Follow The "Zero's Journey" Blog

Facebook Pages:

Facebook.com/thezerosjourney

Facebook.com/drketcham

LinkedIn:
jon m ketcham

Instagram:
failuretalks1

YouTube:
Jon Ketcham
Twitter:
@FailureTalks1

Ask Me Who I Was

Sources:

Success

1.) <u>A Tale of Two Cities</u>, Charles Dickens
2.) <u>Think And Grow Rich</u>, Napoleon Hill p. 55
3.) <u>Meadville Tribune</u>, 9/25/2009
4.) <u>Textbook of Medical Physiology</u>, Guyton Chpt. 5 & 6
5.) <u>Essentials of Strength Training and Conditioning</u>, Baechle pp. 20, 37
6.) <u>Step Into Your Greatness</u>, Les Brown – Live DVD
7.) "Are You Positive?", Steve Jeck, MILO Sept. 2008 ,Vol. 16 No. 2
8.) Jim Rohn Weekly E-zine – July 27, 2009
9.) <u>Fabulously Fit Forever – Expanded</u>, Frank Zane p. 46

Finding Your Purpose, Getting A Life

1.) <u>Man's Search For Meaning</u>, Viktor Frankl p.76
2.) <u>Live Young Forever</u>, Jack LaLanne p.200
3.) Brian Tracy Quote of the Day, 10/15/2009
4.) <u>Maze of Life</u>, Barry Bittman, M.D. and Anthony DeFail, M.P.H. p.10
5.) <u>Man's Search For Meaning</u>, pp71,72,74
6.) <u>The Treasury of Quotes By Jim Rohn</u>, Jim Rohn p.83
7.) Neale Donald Walsch daily quote 10/12/2009

Things Cost Too Much

1.) <u>The Treasury of Quotes by Jim Rohn</u> Jim Rohn p.51
2.) <u>Leading An Inspired Life</u> Jim Rohn p.38
3.) <u>The Power of Focus</u> Jack Canfield, Mark Victor Hansen, Les Hewitt pp.282-287
4.) <u>Secrets of the Millionaire Mind</u> T. Harv Eker p.15
5.) <u>The Success Principles</u> Jack Canfield p.6
6.) <u>In Search of the Invisible Forces</u> George Addair p.25
7.) "The Northern Light" Vol. 41 No. 1 February 2010 p.27
8.) <u>Leading An Inspired Life</u> Jim Rohn pp. 416-418
9.) <u>The Power of Focus</u> Jack Canfield, Mark Victor Hansen, Les Hewit p. 59
10.) <u>The Power of Focus</u> Jack Canfield, Mark Victor Hansen, Les Hewitt p.262
11.) <u>Identity Passport To Freedom – Nine Step Success Process</u> Stedman Graham p.20

Soulmates

1.) <u>Success: Quotes for Achievers</u> Les Brown p.19

Say, "Thank You" and Get Well Sooner:
The Healing Power of Positive Emotions

1.) <u>Think And Grow Rich</u>, Napoleon Hill p. 55
2.) <u>Getting Well Again</u>, O. Carl Simonton, M.D., Stephanie Matthews-Simonton, James L. Creighton p.54
3.) <u>Getting Well Again</u>, p.57
4.) Experience Life magazine, October 2010, "Upgrade Your Brain", p. 56
5.) <u>The Secret</u>, Rhonda Byrne p. 133
6.) <u>Getting Well Again</u>, p. 131

Living A Life With No Regrets

1.) Brian Tracy Quote of the Day, February 3, 2011
2.) <u>Illusions: The Adventures of a Reluctant Messiah</u>, Richard Bach p. 120
3.) <u>The Treasury of Quotes by Jim Rohn</u>, Jim Rohn p. 40
4.) <u>Think And Grow Rich</u>, Napoleon Hill p. 55
5.) Insight of the Day, Bob Proctor, February 17, 2011

Transcendental Living: *Journeys of a Lifetime*

1.) <u>Webster's New Universal Unabridged Dictionary</u>, 1996 edition, p. 2009
2.) <u>Milo</u>, Volume 18, Number 4, March 2011, p. 2
3.) <u>The Meadville Tribune</u>, cryptoquote, April 23, 2011

4.) <u>Leading An Inspired Life</u>, Jim Rohn, p. 71
5.) <u>Leading An Inspired Life</u>, Jim Rohn, p. 72
6.) Neale Donald Walsch – daily e-mail newsletter, April 21, 2011

What's Your Story?

1.) <u>Mr. Magorium's Wonder Emporium</u>, (DVD)
2.) <u>Live Full And Die Empty</u>, Les Brown (DVD)
3.) <u>Live Full And Die Empty</u>, Les Brown (DVD)
4.) <u>Excerpts From The Treasury Of Quotes By Jim Rohn</u>, Jim Rohn p. 22

Soulmates II

1.) <u>www.searchquotes.com</u>
2.) The Book of Positive Quotations by John Cook, p. 270

Finding Your Afflatus

1.) <u>Webster's New Universal Unabridged Dictionary</u>, 1996 edition, p. 34
2.) <u>The Treasury Of Quotes By Jim Rohn</u>, Jim Rohn, p.83
3.) <u>Man's Search For Meaning</u>, Viktor Frankl, p. 76
4.) <u>www.BrainyQuote.com</u>, Michelangelo Quotes
5.) <u>The Power Of Focus</u>, Jack Canfield, Mark Victor Hansen and Les Hewitt, p.159

6.) iContractor1...Constructing Your Perfect Life By Remodeling YOU From The Inside-Out, Dr. Jon M. Ketcham
7.) The Power Of Focus, Jack Canfield, Mark Victor Hansen and Les Hewitt, p.159

Finding Inner Peace Without Caving To Outside Noise!

1.) Wikipedia
2.) Experts Industry Association Conference, November 2011
3.) Live Full & Die Empty (DVD)
4.) Live Full & Die Empty (DVD)

How The Coming Presidential Elections Will Change Your Finances!

1.) Quotationsbook.com/quote/10912/
2.) The Challenge To Succeed, Jim Rohn, Disc 1, Track 13
3.) Man's Search For Meaning, Viktor Frankl p. 66

Roadblocks To Success

1.) Chitty Chitty Bang Bang (DVD)
2.) The Little Engine That Could, Watty Piper
3.) Adapted from The Science of Chiropractic, D.D. Palmer pp. 78-81

Senioritis... Deal With It Now BEFORE It's Too Late!

1.) <u>Secrets Of The Millionaire Mind</u>, T. Harv Eker p. 121
2.) <u>Robert Frost's Poems</u>, New Enlarged Pocket Anthology p. 223

False Prophets, Ostriches & Groupies – The Delusions of Social Media and its Messiahs

1.) Extreme poverty in America: read the UN special monitor's report
Philip Alston, the UN's special rapporteur on extreme poverty and human rights, <u>The Guardian</u>, December 15, 2017
2.) <u>The Diary of a Young Girl</u>, Anne Frank

Dodging the Most Useless Question in the World – How to Stop Languishing & Start Living Again

1.) <u>Quarrel</u>, short-film by Jon D. Ketcham (2014)
2.) <u>To a Mouse</u>, Robert Burns (1785)

Mirrors, Windows, Doors & Light

1.) <u>Secrets Of The Millionaire Mind</u>, T. Harv Eker p.15
2.) <u>Success: Quotes For Achievers</u>, Les Brown p.19
3.) <u>The Law Of Success</u>, Napoleon Hill p.271
4.) <u>Man's Search For Meaning</u>, Viktor Frankl p.66
5.) <u>Count Your Blessings</u>, Dr. John F. Demartini p. 212
6.) <u>In Tune With The Infinite</u>, Ralph Waldo Trine p. 33
7.) <u>Bible</u>, John 14:2
8.) <u>Count Your Blessings</u>, Dr. John F. Demartini p.29
9.) Neale Donald Walsch, daily e-mail newsletter 4/12/2011
10.) <u>Think And Grow Rich</u>, (Fawcett Crest edition, 1960), Napoleon Hill p. 55
11.) <u>Feel the Fear and Do It Anyway</u> ®, Susan Jeffers
12.) <u>The Book Of Positive Quotes</u>, John Cook p. 219
13.) <u>Bible</u>, Genesis 1:27
14.) <u>Bible</u>, John 8:12
15.) <u>Bible</u>, John 10:30
16.) This Date, From Henry David Thoreau's Journal, April 24, 1859
17.) Dr. John F. Demartini, Facebook posting 6/20/2011
18.) <u>Step Into Your Greatness</u>, Les Brown (DVD), track 1 of 7

Ask Me Who I Was

audacious brain farts

Notes

Notes

Notes

Notes

audacious brain farts

Notes

Notes

audacious brain farts

Notes

Notes

audacious brain farts

Notes

Notes

audacious brain farts

Notes